More Praise for *Turnaround Leadership for Higher Education*

"*Turnaround Leadership for Higher Education* offers a new evidence-based perspective on what is needed to generate and sustain 'change-capable' higher education cultures. Above all, it reveals the dire consequences of not acting in the face of relentless pressures on postsecondary institutions. A basically optimistic book, but only if we take and act on its compelling message."—Sharon Bell, senior program developer, L. H. Martin Institute, Graduate School of Education, University of Melbourne

"This book shows us how leaders in higher education can build capacity, engage staff, and bring about the kind of change that is both productive and long-term. Its key lessons are solidly grounded in empirical research. The real issues faced by hundreds of experienced higher education leaders come through with great immediacy, making this an invaluable resource for everyone concerned with the future of higher education."—Richard Johnstone, executive director, Australian Learning & Teaching Council

"The issue of leadership in higher education has never been as important as it is today. *Turnaround Leadership for Higher Education* is timely and impressive while being evidence-based, highly readable, and, above all, practical. The authors' message, that leaders in higher education can be developed, and that there are distinct capabilities associated with successful university leadership, has immediate relevance to all university leaders and managers, academic developers, and directors of HR."—John Dewar, deputy vice chancellor (academic) and provost, Nathan Campus, Griffith University, Australia

"Fullan and Scott's *Turnaround Leadership for Higher Education* is exceedingly timely, important, and rich with wisdom. The authors address the challenge of helping leaders reform higher education—perhaps the toughest reform task of the 25 or so books that Fullan has written. When it comes to understanding leadership in the new age, this book is an out-of-the-ballpark home run. It is absolutely the right message at the right time."—John D. Bransford, Shauna C. Larson University Professor of Education and Psychology, University of Washington

Michael Fullan
Geoff Scott

Turnaround Leadership for Higher Education

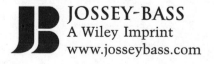

JOSSEY-BASS
A Wiley Imprint
www.josseybass.com

Published by Jossey-Bass
A Wiley Imprint
989 Market Street, San Francisco, CA 94103-1741—www.josseybass.com

Jossey-Bass books and products are available through most bookstores. To contact Jossey-Bass directly call our Customer Care Department within the U.S. at 800-956-7739, outside the U.S. at 317-572-3986, or fax 317-572-4002.

Jossey-Bass also publishes its books in a variety of electronic formats. Some content that appears in print may not be available in electronic books.

Cataloging-in-publication data has been applied for.
ISBN: 978-0-4704-7204-0

Credits:
List on p. 152 from David M. Herold and Donald B. Fedor, *Change the way you lead change: Leadership Strategies that really work.* Copyright © 2008 by the Board of Trustees of the Leland Stanford Jr. University. All rights reserved. Used with permission of Stanford University Press, www.sup.org.

Printed in the United States of America
FIRST EDITION
HB Printing   10 9 8 7 6 5 4 3 2 1

The Jossey-Bass
Higher and Adult Education Series

Contents

Preface

It has been observed that elementary school teachers love their children, high school teachers love their subjects, and university professors love themselves. We know all three groups, and there is more than a little truth to these generalizations. It seems that the more you move up the education hierarchy, the more difficult it is to bring about change. Universities, with all their brainpower, are much more resistant to change than many other institutions. Universities are great at studying and recommending change for others, but when it comes to themselves, that is another matter. The university stance reminds us of the Dilbert cartoon: "Change is good. You go first."

There is no doubt, as we will see, that the pressure for change from sources outside the university is mounting. For us this provides an opportunity for universities to redefine themselves in ways that deeply enhance many of their original purposes. This book tackles the question of how universities can effect change from within—what should be the focus of the turnaround and what leadership capabilities will be needed to lead this transformation.

To do this, change leaders at all levels of the university will need to grapple with both the content and the process of change. Relative to the latter, we have each studied and participated in major change initiatives in higher education, elementary and secondary schools, and government-led reforms, and have linked them to strong literature on change management in all sectors of society (see especially, Fullan, 2008a, and Scott, Coates, & Anderson, 2008). There is a solid change knowledge base available which amounts to figuring out how to stimulate and integrate strong moral purpose and equally strong partnerships and relationships inside and outside the institution—conviction and connection in equal measure. We draw on this considerable knowledge about the dynamics of change throughout the book.

The context of change is of key importance. This relates not only to how universities keep in step with a rapidly changing environment but, more important, how universities as knowledge organizations evolve and change within this environment. This requires new ways of thinking organizationally about knowledge and learning—how to grow it, link it, and share it. This includes knowledge about what the most productive focus should be in learning, research, engagement, and service, what generates productive learning and retains students, how to make sure these objectives are successfully and consistently put into practice, and how well the university is performing.

One of the most pressing problems in higher education is not just access but completion rates for those entering four-year programs, which have fallen steadily in the U.S. over the past 30 years. Currently, just 40% of those entering (half of that rate for disadvantaged students) from four-year programs graduate—a disturbingly low rate. Our proposals, if implemented, will reverse this trend by making the learning experience of students more meaningful and valuable.

The content of change is, of course, critically important, but how do you go beyond a list of core purposes? We need above all a simple but powerful expression of the university in the 21st century, one that is comprehensive and integrated. We will take the three core purposes of the university: research, teaching, and external service or engagement (the latter defined broadly to include reciprocal partnerships with the field designed for improvement). But we need an integrator—something that serves all three purposes synergistically. In one sense, what all three purposes have (or should have) in common is knowledge. Knowledge development and use is what universities should be good at. But it turns out that they are not, except in isolated pockets. Walk through any university and you see scores of over- and underconceptualized practice.

The integrator for us is the teaching and learning that continually fosters the development and use of knowledge linked to research and practice (engagement and service). This demands a careful understanding of the role of knowledge. The essence of knowledge as an integrator is how it can combine critical analysis and applied judgment to deal constructively with the issues of the day. Progress on this matter is best made through reforming teaching in universities, not just in the professional schools but across arts and sciences. One of the richest research laboratories of the university of the future will be the *research on the practice of teaching and learning* and its central role in achieving beneficial social, economic, and environmental change.

However, teaching and learning as applied judgment in a narrow sense is not our main focus. We have bigger fish to fry. This book is about how certain leadership capabilities and change-capable cultures in higher education must mirror each other—for the benefit of students and their futures, for the benefit of postsecondary institutions, and for the benefit of society. Moreover, we identify a tremendous and powerful convergence in the nature of leadership for change that applies to *all* institutions. As we will show, successful leaders, whatever the organization, listen, link, and lead. In so doing, they bring about change not by implementing given visions from their powerbase but by reconciling factors and divisions to achieve reform that motivates people from different groups to unify their change efforts. Nothing is more crucial for the future of civilization than resolving differences among people in a manner that leads to sustaining and enhancing the social, political, and physical environment.

Postsecondary institutions are especially well placed to help lead the future, but they are currently falling far short of their potential in this regard. Institutions of higher education can, must, and should model productive, change-capable cultures. If you purport to make learning your forte, you better deliver on it by exemplifying the highest possible standard. This is the future of higher education.

In Chapter 1 we set the context by reiterating what many others have described as the mounting pressures and challenges facing universities. Chapter 2 reviews the existing barriers and failed strategies used so far to address the challenges of change. In chapter 3 we set out the new agenda. Some scholars have begun to map out this terrain and it is exciting but daunting. In Chapter 4 we use our change knowledge to identify steps that need to be taken for building quality and capacity around the new agenda. None of this will happen unless we understand what leadership capacity entails (Chapter 5). Chapter 6 takes up the topic of how best to select and develop leaders at all levels of higher education. Finally, in Chapter 7, we revisit what it means to lead and keep on leading. All of this involves merging leadership and change-capable cultures.

Our database comes from three main sources: first, from the direct study of quality learning processes and outcomes; second, from leading and studying change within our own universities and in elementary, secondary, and postsecondary institutions in several countries; and third, from our review of the change literature in the public and private sectors as well as our own theories of action (see Fullan, 2001, 2008a, and Scott, 1999).

In terms of our direct study of the problem, we draw substantially on the Australian Learning and Teaching Council (ALTC) report, *Learning Leaders in Times of Change* (Scott, Coates, & Anderson, 2008). The ALTC study was based on the interactive input of 513 academic leaders (presidents, vice presidents, provosts, pro or deputy vice chancellors, deans, department heads, and directors of learning and teaching units) from 20 Australian universities who responded to a leadership survey. Six hundred additional senior university staff participated in workshops and discussions conducted in Australia, Canada, New Zealand, South Africa, the United Kingdom, and the United States during 2007 and 2008 to review the results of that survey and its implications. The ALTC study identified the capabilities that characterize effective academic leaders in a range of roles and has produced resources to develop and monitor their leadership capabilities. It has identified that the core focus for leadership in the current, highly volatile operating context faced by our universities has to be on achieving effective change management and implementation.

In the final analysis, this book is for leaders inside and outside universities who wish to respond in focused proactive, ways to the many challenges and expectations facing universities—indeed, *Turnaround Leadership for Higher Education* is about societal and global development.

Acknowledgments

This book is the outcome of more than three decades' active engagement in designing, delivering, and studying turnaround projects in schools and in postsecondary and higher education. In writing this book, we are indebted to the many hundreds of practitioners around the world with whom we have taken this journey. In a very important sense, it is the combined story of us all—what follows has been built from real-world experience and our collective consideration of the key lessons it has taught us about leadership and change. We have learned from the best and thank them all for the lessons of change that they have taught us.

We especially thank David Brightman, our editor at Jossey-Bass, who made several strategic suggestions that made this book much stronger and sharper, and Claudia Cuttress who put together the manuscript in its various forms into a final product.

About the Authors

Michael Fullan is professor emeritus at the Ontario Institute for Studies in Education at the University of Toronto and is special adviser on education to Dalton McGuinty, the Premier of Ontario. He holds honorary doctorates from the University of Edinburgh, Scotland, and from Nipissing University, Canada.

Fullan served as dean of the faculty of education at the University of Toronto from 1988 to 2003, leading two major organizational transformations, including a merger of two large schools of education. He is currently working as adviser and consultant on several major education reform initiatives around the world.

He bases his work on research and practice drawn from both the public and private sectors, finding an increasing convergence in the best of this literature. He has written several best sellers on leadership and change that have been translated into several languages. His latest book is *The Six Secrets of Change* also published by Jossey-Bass.

Visit his website at www.michaelfullan.ca.

Geoff Scott is pro-vice chancellor at the University of Western Sydney, Australia, and provost of its Penrith Campus.

Over the past thirty years, Scott has led or studied major change projects in schools and in postsecondary and higher education in

Australia and in several countries including South Africa, Cambodia, New Zealand, Canada, and Scandinavia. He has served on a range of ministerial advisory panels, produced commissioned reports for national reviews, and undertaken a number of national and international research studies on university student learning, change management, and leadership. In 2000 he was elected as a fellow of the Australian College of Education for his contributions to post-secondary and higher education, and in 2007 was the recipient of the Australian Higher Education Quality Award. He is a member of the board of directors of the Australian Council for Educational Research.

Turnaround Leadership
for Higher Education

Universities and the Challenges of the 21st Century

A word about where we are heading. It is necessary, and in fact easy, to identify the growing list of change forces in the environment that are challenging universities with ferocious intensity. This chapter lays out these dynamic factors. This critical analysis turns out to be simultaneously the strength of university thinking and its Achilles heel. A core theme of this book is that critical analysis does not tell you enough about critical solutions. Put another way, knowing the challenges intimately says very little about strategic action. We first set out the challenges and then return at the end of the chapter to the matter of why we find this level of analysis seriously limiting for turning around universities.

The literature on higher education over the past decade is replete with statements like the following. For example, from a U.S. perspective:

> . . . higher education is operating in a new environment, perhaps for the first time since the immediate post-World War II era. The ground is shifting. Colleges and universities are confronting new types of students—younger and more technology-driven, as well as older and more career-driven. They are confronting unprecedented com-

petition, aggressive accountability demands and a view of operating in a global context. And they are doing all of this with less direct funding. . . . The greatest challenges facing higher education today (are): student engagement; institutional accountability; revenue generation; (and) globalization. . . . All of the education leaders we interviewed understand the importance of more market-oriented, student-centered and businesslike management and accountability strategies, while preserving their academic mission, focus and values. [Segall & Freedman, 2007, pp. 1-2]

And from a European perspective, Brenda Gourley, vice chancellor of the Open University, observes:

I believe, and I am not alone, that we are witnessing a seismic shift in higher education. . . embracing the unprecedented opportunities offered by the global technology-fuelled society and embracing collaboration are the major strategies for survival in this new world. . . (However, we) have to ask ourselves some tough questions about the production of some of our teaching materials, not only because our model is an expensive one but also because it is relatively slow in a world growing so accustomed to the swift satisfaction of consumer needs. . .Otherwise, while we are all talking about diploma supplements and Erasmus programs and whether or not we believe in quality assurance, China and India are going to come and take our lunch. [Gourley, 2007]

Below we identify five broad change forces and six specific to higher education. These underpin the observations made above.

Broad	Higher Education Related
Global stresses	Opening of access
New world players	Changes in funding and pressure to generate new sources of revenue
Exit of Baby Boomers	Export market and new growing competition
IT revolution	User pay and changing patterns of participation
Fractious divisions	Changing expectations of students and growing diversity
	Maintaining standards

Broader Change Forces

Some of the developments that have unfolded over recent decades are not specific to universities but nevertheless have profound implications for them.

Global Stresses

The impact of global warming and the emergence of environmental (and social) sustainability have emerged as key political national and international research and learning themes for the new century. Thomas Homer-Dixon (2006) calls these trends "tectonic stresses" that include population stress, energy stress, environmental stress (land, water, forests, fisheries), climate stress, and economic stress (the ever-widening income gap between the rich and poor).

The global financial crisis in late 2008 is an example of how significant such tectonic stresses can be for higher education. As a result of the rapid drop in the value of stock markets at that time, the endowments of U.S. higher education institutions (said to be upwards of $400 billion) were hard hit, with falls in their value reported to be 20% or higher. With this came pressures to cut state budgets for higher education, to increase tuition fees and reduce aid, to freeze recruitment or lay off staff, and a slowdown in some college building programs. There were also reports that the solvency of some smaller colleges was threatened. This added to the challenges faced by the new Obama presidency, which had boosting access to colleges as one plank of its platform (*Chronicle of Higher Education*, 2008; Lewin, 2008).

There is also the rapid emergence of the new, "connected" global economy, including the emergence of large multinational corporations that operate beyond state jurisdiction resulting in a rapid growth in cross-border transactions. "One of the major transforming factors, enabled by advances in communications and information technology, is that of globalization through the mobility of ideas, capital, and people. In this new context, we are witnessing new formations of globally networked companies and cities and new roles for research universities" (Group of Eight, 2007, p. 14).

Prior to globalization, the United States dominated the world economy. In recent years, however, the U.S. share of global gross domestic product (GDP) is reported to be shrinking. For example, the *New York Times* (Gross, 2007) reported: "According to Goldman Sachs, the United States' share of global gross domestic product fell to 27.7% in 2006 from 31% in 2000. In the same period, the share of Brazil, Russia, India and China—the rapidly growing emerging markets referred to as the BRICs—rose to 11% from 7.8%. China alone accounts for 5.4%." The U.S. Department of Agriculture figures vary slightly but are in the same direction (U.S. Department of Agriculture, 2007).

The Emergence of New World Players

While U.S. higher education has long been admired internationally, its continued preeminence is no longer something we can take for granted. The rest of the world is catching up and by some measures the U.S. has already been overtaken. It has slipped to 12th in higher education attainment (Segall & Freedman, 2007, p. 9). Prominent examples of the new world players economically as well as educationally are India and China. These are countries that see investment in higher education as a key element in their strategic development and have experienced a startling increase in higher education participation rates over the past five years. They are also dramatically improving the quality of their education: "The European Commissioner for Education, Jan Figel, told *The Times* Newspaper (May 2007) that he expects Chinese and Indian universities to overtake UK, French and German universities in international rankings within a decade unless they work hard to improve quality and access" (*Campus Review*, May 29, 2007, p. 7).

There are also significant developments in Europe—in particular the creation of the European Higher Education Area through the implementation of the Bologna Process: "The Bologna Declaration of June 1999 has put in motion a series of reforms needed to make European Higher Education more compatible and comparable, more competitive and more attractive for Europeans and for students and scholars from other continents" (http://www.ond. vlaanderen.be/hogeronderwijs/bologna/). The Bologna reforms involve 46 European countries (http://www.ond.vlaanderen.be/ hogeronderwijs/bologna/pcao/index.htm), and the process includes harmonization of degrees into a three-cycle system, the establishment of a European Qualifications Framework for lifelong learning (EQF), a range of quality assurance measures (ENQA), greater transparency in qualifications (EUROPASS), setting up a European Credit Transfer System (ECTS), and the production of a common diploma supplement system. The exact nature and extent of the impact that the initiative will have on higher education systems around the world will become clear over the next decade. However, many countries outside of Europe are already looking in detail at how best to respond.

Exit of the Baby Boomers

The imminent retirement of the Baby Boomer generation will have a dramatic impact on the staff and leadership of our universities over the coming decade. As Graham Hugo, an Australian Research Council Federation fellow and professor of demography has noted, universities will lose between one-fifth and one-third of academic staff members by 2015 (Hugo, 2005, p. 20). In some universities, it is predicted that up to half of their leadership and a significant proportion of line staff may retire in the next five years. Recruitment is going to be excessively difficult as this will occur simultaneously across all developed countries, and the 1970s strategy of filling the gap through recruitment of academics from overseas will not work.

Baby Boomer retirement, combined with other change forces, will have an impact on the education policy priorities for the new Obama administration in the U.S. As Arthur Levine observed:

> The Obama higher education platform focused on five critical issues: access, affordability, research, economic development, and international competitiveness. . .
>
> A number of pressures will now require the new president to rethink this array of important proposals because he won't have the resources to carry out this agenda. First, discretionary dollars will be eaten up by the $800 billion bailout, additional federal funding for economic relief, the continuing cost of the Iraq war, and declines in tax revenues. Second, support for education has diminished as a priority for the American people. . . Third, . . .the sheer size of the Baby Boom generation ensures that every politician running for any office, from dogcatcher to president of the United States, quickly develops a platform that emphasizes Boomers' interests. As a result, elder care, health insurance and Social Security have become the new priority—and will likely continue to overshadow education in the years ahead, since

the first Boomers reached retirement age this year.
[Levine, 2008]

The IT Revolution

How to handle the relentless development of communication and
information technologies, their rapid influx into our daily lives, the
exponential growth in computing power, and the rapid growth in Inter-
net speeds are posing major challenges for universities and colleges.

The IT revolution is creating new expectations and opportunities for how students want to and can learn. It questions whether
higher education should remain campus-based or become more "distributed," especially given the increased difficulty of travel to large
cities and the potential for people to work productively for at least
part of their week at home. Already, traditional universities are no
longer viewed as the sole, or even key, repository of leading-edge
knowledge or necessarily as being the best place to access it. The
University of Phoenix (http://www.phoenix.edu/) is the premier
example of thriving online and distance learning. With a reported
enrollment of 350,000 students, 200 campuses, and over 100 degree
programs at the bachelor, master's, and doctoral levels, it is the
largest private university in North America.

However, there is clear evidence that simply putting a university online is no guarantee for success. As Richard Garrett,
deputy director of the Observatory on Borderless Higher Education, noted in 2004 when discussing the expensive collapse of the
UK e-University: "Along with NYU Online, Scottish Knowledge
and Fathom, UKeU has now failed. Others, such as Universitas 21
Global and Global University Alliance, stumble on with no evidence of particular success. Meanwhile, universities across the world
are gradually moving online—both on and off campus—to varying
extents, building slowly and learning all the time. This may be the
end for UKeU but for online learning it is only the beginning (Garrett, 2004, p. 3).

When commenting on the failure of the UK's Open University in America, David Kirp (2003) identified some of the reasons why a purely online model won't work: "With so much attention focused on high-tech and quick killings, little notice was paid to offering something of value (p. 186). . . advising, counseling, and grading were done on-line (thereby negating the very secret of the OU's success in the UK—the support offered by its counselors, tutors and group meetings) (p. 199) . . . the network of personal relationships between students and their tutors may matter as much as the thick packet of readings and video and audio cassettes that students receive" (p. 192).

The issues of access and equity, including those associated with the digital divide, continue to create moral and political dilemmas. As Sir John Daniel, chair of the Commonwealth of Learning, recently observed at the Council for Higher Education Accreditation's International Commission Conference in Washington, DC: "To date the growth of higher education in the developing world has been constrained by various factors, notably cost. But today spreading connectivity, allied with the massive creation of open educational resources based on open-source technology, could create the radical reduction in costs necessary for higher education to serve the four billion people at the bottom of the world's economic pyramid. Were that to happen it would generate over a hundred million more students" (Daniel, 2007).

Fractious Divisions

Divisions in societies seem to be on the rise: the growing gap between the poor and the rich, the differences between Generation X and Generation Y, the divide between the left and the right, and so on. A microcosm of this development can be seen in universities. Even before the economic crisis and the 2008 U.S. presidential election, the University of California's survey of 270,000 entering undergraduates at 400 colleges across the country uncovered an interesting trend. The proportion of students who identified as being liberal

(28%) and conservative (24%) was the highest in decades. Fewer than half said they are "middle of the road," the lowest percentage measured since 1970 (Powers, 2007). Thus, the middle is leaking to both the left and the right.

We argue that change for the future should no longer be one group dominating another (unless you want a civil war). And it is equally clear that "split the difference" compromises would be disastrous. This is the heart of turnaround leadership. It is not about compromise or about overpowering each other. It is not even about transcending differences. It is about confronting, reconciling, and *fulfilling* disparate aspirations through unifying experiences and win-win scenarios; and doing this against clear, explicit, and widely shared criteria on what constitutes a civil society (Cox, 1995) and a clear understanding of what constitutes progress, that is, change in a positive direction. The capability to lead this process will be as critical for university leaders as it will be for leaders of nations.

Change Forces Specific to Higher Education

Other changes over the past quarter century have been more directly connected to the daily operations of the university and have brought with them a wide range of pressures on their funding, support, and operation.

Opening Up of Access

In the developed world, the proportion of the population gaining access to higher education opportunities has grown dramatically since the 1970s, and the trend is continuing. For example, the OECD (2008, Table A2.5 at http://ocde.p4.siteinternet.com/publications/doifiles/962008041P1G002.xls) reports that entry rates for type A tertiary education programs (programs leading to advanced degrees) over the period 2000 to 2006 grew from 59% to 84% in Australia, from 67% to 76% in Sweden, 43% to 64% in the U.S., and from 47%

to 57% in the U.K. These entry rates are calculated as percentages of school leavers attending higher education during their lifetime (see: http://stats.oecd.org/glossary/detail.asp?ID=5359).

In the developing world the growth in higher education participation rates has been equally impressive, albeit with some notable exceptions:

> There is no doubt about the demand. For two decades worldwide enrollment growth has exceeded the most optimistic forecasts. A milestone of 100 million enrollments was passed some years ago, and an earlier forecast of 120 million students by 2020 looks likely to be reached by 2010. Indeed, if part-time students are counted, numbers have already passed 130 million. Growth is, if anything, accelerating as more governments see the rapid expansion of higher education as key to their transition to developed country status.
>
> Thus in China enrollments doubled between 2000 and 2003. By 2005, with 16 million students, China had overtaken the U.S. as the world's largest higher education system. Malaysia also illustrates the trend. It plans to increase enrollments in higher education by 166 percent in the next four years, from 600,000 to 1.6 million, in order to achieve developed-nation participation rates. Mauritius has recently passed legislation to create a third university for its 1.2 million people, having added a second only five years ago.
>
> Growth has been rapid in other developing countries as well—but usually from a very low base. Across the world there is a massive disparity in the higher education participation rates of people between 18 and 23 years old (known as Age Participation Rates, or APRs). APRs of around 50 percent are now seen in many developed countries, whereas in numerous countries in South Asia

and Sub-Saharan Africa they languish below 10 percent. [Daniel, 2007]

Along with the rapid increase in the percentage of the population attending university in both developed and developing countries has come the challenge of managing the transition of many of the students who are first in their family to attend university. These people are often uncertain about tertiary study, but, once alerted to how university learning works, they perform well. However, this transition assistance comes at a cost and is putting additional pressure on cash-strapped institutions.

Changes in Funding and Pressure to Generate New Sources of Revenue

> We simply need a more stable and secure level of resources. It is a fact that in our state, like most, that Medicare, K–12 and prisons are going to take increasingly larger percentages of the budget, while higher education is seen as being more part of the discretionary budget. [Harvey Perlman, chancellor, University of Nebraska, Lincoln, cited in Segall & Freedman, 2007, p. 7]

The dramatic rise in participation rates has created increased pressure on funding for higher education, especially from state sources. For example, over the past 25 years there has been a significant decrease in government funding per capita for higher education students in many countries. In the U.S., Kirp reports "nationwide between 1980 and 2000, the share of universities' operating expenses paid for by state tax dollars was cut by 30%" (2003, pp. 131–132). The Organisation for Economic Co-operation and Development (OECD) (2007 and 2008) *Education at a Glance* reports show that over the period 1995 to 2005 the percentage of government funding per capita in higher education in the U.K. dropped by 13.1%, in Australia by 17%, in the U.S., by 2.7%, and in Canada by 1.5%. "Ever since Harvard College and the College of William and Mary opened their doors over three centuries ago, money has been a pressing concern and the need for a useful and usable education has been a theme in American public policy. . . What is new, and troubling, is the raw power that money directly exerts over so many aspects of higher education. . . the American university has been busily reinventing itself in response to intense competitive pressures" (Kirp, 2003, p. 3).

A headline story in the Higher Education Supplement of *The Australian Newspaper* indicates the impact this trend is having in countries other than the U.S. "Ferocious competition, a move into less specialized courses and more local students on full fees are expected as a shake-out sparked by a (recently announced) 40 percent cut in federal funding for university business courses. . . Many business faculties say the move spells an end to the era of growth" (Higher Education Supplement, 2007).

It must be noted that there has always been considerable variation between countries on the extent to which funding for higher education research comes from government, charitable, or business sources. For example, the U.S. has a strong tradition of funding for higher education through a range of charitable foundations and a culture of giving to one's alma mater. In other countries, this is not the case.

The per capita decrease in state funding has triggered a parallel pressure for universities to generate new sources of income. The drop in the proportion of higher education funding coming from government and the concomitant pressure to generate alternative sources of income has been severely felt in some countries. For example, over the decade 1995 to 2005, the percentage of public expenditure on higher education in Australia fell from 64.8% percent to 47.8%; in the U.K. from 80% to 66.9%; and from a much lower starting point in the U.S., from 37.4% to 34.7%. In Canada it has been relatively stable at around 55% to 56%, whereas in Ireland it has grown from 69.7% to 84%. In Finland and Sweden it has remained relatively high (OECD 2007, 2008).

This has led universities in many countries to focus on profit and commodification of knowledge and its marketing, rather than on the traditional conception of a university as a community of scholars securely funded by the state whose aim is to create new knowledge and seek the truth. David Kirp (2003) suggests the way this pressure has played itself out in U.S. higher education:

> Entrepreneurial ambition, which used to be regarded in academe as a necessary evil, has become a virtue. . . The new vocabulary of customers and stakeholders, niche marketing and branding and winner-take-all, embodies this shift in the higher education "industry". . . Each department is a "revenue center," each student a customer, each professor an entrepreneur, each party a "stakeholder" and each institution a seeker after profit, whether in money capital or intellectual capital. . . Opting out of the fray by fleeing the market is not a realistic possibility. . . maintaining communities of scholars is not a concern of the market. [pp. 4, 261]

Because of this trend, a new range of income-generating ventures, many with a much higher risk profile than that usually associated with a university, has emerged. Risks associated with such ventures include having to deal with uncertain international and local full-fee paying student markets, taking financial responsibility for the commercialization of research or teaching, and holding legal liability for new entities.

In countries where universities operate under an act of parliament, the move to generate university income from these less certain and more risk-prone sources has triggered high levels of government concern about its own legal liability for failed financial ventures. This, in turn, has led to the introduction of a wide range of risk management measures including a rapid increase in government monitoring, auditing, reporting requirements; shifts of legal liability to the governing bodies of universities; and a wide range of external quality monitoring, evaluation and assurance systems, and controlling legislation.

Rapid Growth in the Higher Education Export Market and Growing Competition in All Markets

A key new source of income over the past decade for many higher education systems has been the "higher education export market"— the enrollment of international students at a university either onshore or offshore via an in-country partner or at a satellite campus. Table 1.1, compiled from a triangulated set of sources (Bashir, 2007; *Education Travel Magazine*, 2008; Gee, 2007; Institute of International Education, 2007; Larson, Martin, & Morris, 2002; Reserve Bank Bulletin, 2008; and Spencer, 2007), shows the dramatic increase in the income from this source in many countries.

At a transnational education conference in May 2007, the chief executive of a higher education quality agency observed, when discussing the way the General Agreement on Trade and Services (GATS) is encouraging free trade in the higher education export market, that: "What is new is that higher education is now seen as a service commodity for profit that can be exported and imported. Furthermore the import-export divide is breaking down" (Scott et al., 2008, p. 35). At the same conference, it was reported that

Table 1.1. Higher education export trends (foreign students) by main exporting countries, 1989–2007 (U.S. $ billion)

Country/Year	1989	1999	2005	2007
United States	$4.6	$9.6	$14.1	$14.5
United Kingdom	$2.2	$4.1	$6.0	$9.0*
Australia	$0.6	$2.0	$5.5	$10.4
Canada	$0.5	$0.6	$1.6	$4.0
New Zealand	N/A	$0.3	$1.0	$1.4

*2006 data

U.S. regional accreditation boards are now being invited to accredit university programs in other countries in order to improve the national and international marketability of these programs.

There are suggestions that the international student market will continue to grow at about 6% per annum into the foreseeable future. However, the pattern of growth may be quite different from that of the past decade. One new feature is the tendency, as domestic fees escalate, for students from highly developed countries to choose to take all or part of their degree overseas. This tendency for two-way internationalization in such countries is seen by many to be a desirable development. However, it may have an effect on the bottom line for some universities as traditional student markets from developing countries find an increasing range of countries offering to take them in and as the quality and availability of their own home country operations grow rapidly. At the cheaper end of the international student market, online learning providers are also expected to make significant incursions. However, having said this, predicting accurately the future of the higher education export market remains excessively tricky.

The opening up of the higher education sector to market forces in many countries has seen a rapid influx of private local and international providers who anticipate that large profits can be made from high student fees. This, along with relatively low unemployment rates in a number of developed countries, has seen many universities struggling (often for the first time) to meet their load targets. This, in turn, has had an effect on their bottom line and, in some instances, has seen the closure of faculties or departments with significant staff redundancies. In short, there is no longer any safe domestic or international market and, as a consequence, there are no safe academic departments or jobs.

> Around the world higher education systems are being re-
> shaped through greater competition among established
> institutions, the growth of new providers, including not-

for-profit and proprietary providers, and the growing capacity of on-line learning. There are multiple ways of obtaining qualifications, such as through product vendors, professional associations, and the training houses of global corporations. Additionally some non-university research institutions are seeking authority to offer degrees. . . . (In countries like Australia). . . recently amended national protocols for the approval of higher education providers will facilitate the entry of new competitors. [Group of Eight, 2007, p. 18]

User Pays and Changing Patterns of Participation

With the growth of the "user pays" philosophy for higher education and the significant increase in the fees paid by the student, a student-as-consumer movement has rapidly taken off. This, as noted previously, has led to students being prepared to shift institutions if they do not experience the quality and value-for-money they expect, something which can have a direct and negative impact on the university's bottom line.

For example, if a full-fee-paying student leaves a particular institution at the end of year one in a three-year program, the university loses the remaining two years' fee income—around $30,000 in countries like Australia. Lose just three students on this basis and you lose one annual staff salary. The student-as-consumer trend is also now resulting in a growth in truth in advertising litigation against universities, as students sue postsecondary institutions under provisions of statutes like contract law for not delivering what was promised in their prospectus. There are numerous examples of litigation against universities around the world (see, for example, *University Affairs Canada*, 2008).

In some countries, more and more students are enrolled full time but are working a significant number of hours per week. For example, a 2006 Australian Vice Chancellor's Committee student finance survey (James, Bexley, Devlin, & Marginson, 2007) found that, consistent with the findings of previous studies, the typical Australian university student in 2006 was undertaking considerable paid work during the semester: 70.6% of full-time undergraduates reported working during the semester and, on average, these students were working 14.8 hours per week. One in every six full-time undergraduate students who worked during the semester reported working more than 20 hours per week. More than one-third of the nation's full-time university students—35.2%—were working at least 13 hours per week during the semester. Similar trends show that 41.8% of all part-time students were working at least 38 hours per week—in effect, full-time paid employment. This trend is shaping a quite different set of expectations about university studies and ease of access to programs compared with even a decade ago.

Changing Expectations for a New Generation of Students and Growing Diversity

Unlike earlier generations, it is estimated that Generation Y may have up to 20 jobs over their lifetimes. This creates a profound challenge for how universities structure their programs and for their flexibility and responsiveness. It creates decision-making dilemmas around how specifically focused programs should be, whether helping students learn how to learn should be the focus, and to what extent students want to or should complete the bulk of their higher education before they start their careers. This is not a new dilemma, but the current context throws its importance into sharp relief.

Sally Nimon (2007) identifies the distinguishing characteristics of Generation Y—the so-called millennial generation of higher education students born after 1980. The focus is on how their expectations of university study can differ from older generations. The study by Krause, Hartley, James, and McInnis (2005) of the extent and nature of Generation Y's use of new technologies also indicates that the old transmission modes of learning used in the traditional university learning paradigm do not resonate with younger students.

> Millennial tertiary students have been raised in an environment very different from that of their predecessors and this has fostered a distinct set of experiences, expectations and characteristics, many of which have significant implications for higher education. While it is not yet clear exactly what approaches *will* work with this group there is sufficient evidence to suggest that practices that were successful with Baby Boomers and Generation Xers are likely to fail with their children and younger siblings. Millennials are the future, both literally and figuratively, and it is worth our while to invest in ways to bring them to their full potential. [Nimon, 2007, p. 40]

Nimon's discussion of the implications for higher education suggests, for example, that Generation Y students:

- Can have a quite different interpretation of what access and a timely response mean compared to older generations

- Not only expect an institutional response to their concerns but expect it within a rapid timeframe that institutions may not traditionally be structured to achieve

- May be reluctant to engage in long-term planning and tend to focus on the more immediate benefits of their education

- Have limited instructional loyalty and will readily shift institutions if not happy

- Are likely to have different attitudes to Web-based plagiarism and knowledge

- Can expect to be catered to and may not be as self-reliant as previous generations

- May not comprehend the notion of standards of achievement and expect a pass for anything they submit, irrespective of its quality

- Use peer group references and word of mouth to decide where to enroll rather than traditional marketing techniques, making it vital that currently enrolled Millennials have a positive tertiary experience. [pp. 36–39]

The important role played by the peer group for this generation can be seen in the widespread use of online sites like Bored of Studies or MySpace to discuss which university to go to and how they perform.

Handling the challenge posed by this generation of "digital natives" is now front and center for higher education. For example, one of the most popular sessions at the 2007 annual meeting of academic librarians in Washington, DC, was on how to help students who have learned many of their information gathering and analysis skills from video games apply that knowledge in the library. Speakers said that gaming skills are in many ways representative of a broader cultural divide between today's college students and the librarians who hope to assist them.

As George M. Needham (2007), vice president for member services of the Online Computer Library Center, observed, this does not mean that college libraries should "tear up the stacks to put in arcades," but it does mean that they need to rethink many assumptions. "The librarian as information priest is as dead as Elvis," Needham said. "The whole 'gestalt' of the academic library has been set up like a church," he said, with various parts of a reading room acting like "the stations of the cross," all leading up to the "altar of the reference desk," where "you make supplication and if you are found worthy, you will be helped" (Jaschik, 2007). Some have likened the current challenge in this area as being akin to people brought up with 33-RPM vinyl records trying to teach people who are used to working with MP3 files.

Amidst the above changing expectation is the growing diversity of societies along with large gaps in participation rates across ethnic groups. In the U.S., there are just as many African Americans in prisons as there are in universities. African Americans and Latinos are substantially underrepresented in higher education and far more likely to drop out from college once they enter. For example, in California, estimates of the percentage of students completing a bachelor's degree range from 52% for whites to 5% for blacks to 19% for Latinos (Valverde, 2008, p. 111).

Maintaining and Enhancing Standards

With the dramatic increase in participation rates and the drive to bring in new sources of income have come questions about a drop in standards and quality. Recently many universities have become increasingly interested in assuring the consistency and quality of what they do across all classes and campuses (see Bollaert et al., 2007). Our book will have much to say about quality processes and standards in today's and tomorrow's universities.

Challenges in Perspective

We have just reviewed in broad strokes the types of challenges facing universities. It is important to recognize that the challenges identified above do not operate independently. Instead they both feed into and off each other. These change forces and the concomitant crisis are echoed across the recent literature in higher education. Peter Smith (2004) talks about the "quiet crisis" in U.S. higher education, which he defines as the reliance on a classic academic model that "flies in the face of what we know about how people learn, the opportunities that technology presents to transform the educational enterprise and our historic record of failure with a rapidly diversifying population" (p. xix). Newman, Couturier, and Scurry (2004) refer to "rhetoric, reality, and the risks of the market." They document in detail "the new competition" and lament the lack of response on the part of universities to focus on standards, commenting that "it is a higher education system that fiercely defends a rhetoric of excellence and public purpose while the reality slips" (p. 66). Gappa, Austen, and Trice (2007) also describe higher education's changed context in terms similar to those we have been using in this chapter. They identify four themes: (1) fiscal constraints and increased competition; (2) calls for accountability; (3) growing enrollment and increasing diversity of students; and (4) the rise of the information age (p. 1).

The literature boils down to two conclusions. One, universities must revisit and redefine their public purpose in light of the new change forces. Second, many universities do not have the focus and wherewithal to take action. The biggest barriers may be within the university.

Relative to public purpose, Newman et al.'s (2004) distillation is as good as any:

- Improve the quality of learning so as to ensure the skills and knowledge required for the workplace.

- Improve the quality of learning so as to reflect the skills, knowledge and commitment for active participation in civic and social life.

- Provide access and attainment to all races, ages, ethnicities and socioeconomic backgrounds.

- Serve as an avenue of social mobility for lower SES and minority citizens.

- Serve as the location for open debate of critical and controversial issues.

- Support the development of high quality teachers and leaders of elementary and secondary schools.

- Undertake research and scholarship that is trustworthy, open and of strong quality.

- Bring the benefit of knowledge and skills to the community through outreach, partnerships and service. [pp. 83–84]

The Moral Imperative for Universities

Much of the above traces the links between the exponential changes in the operating environment of universities and their financial viability. However, there is an equally profound set of factors that relate not just to the financial benefits to the individual (PriceWaterhouseCoopers, 2007) but to the personal, moral, and societal benefits of higher education. Retention at university matters. It matters morally, as we know the life chances of people who complete a degree are dramatically improved. And it matters nationally, as the higher the education level of the population, the greater the nation's levels of productivity and innovation. In this regard the current track record in many countries is not good. The new problem in higher education is not just to improve access but *completion* rates. In a recent study of Institutional Transformation it was reported that in the U.S. "national statistics showed that it took nearly 7 years, on average, to finish a 4-year degree. And a growing number of students failed ever to complete the degree. According to ACT's ongoing study of retention and completion, BA/BS completion rates at 4-year public colleges have been falling from a high of 52.8% in 1986 to a 20-year low of 39.5% in 2005" (Pennsylvania State University et al., 2006, p. 49).

In short, the new challenge for higher education is not simply to gain students but retain them to graduation. In a detailed historical analysis, two Harvard economists (Goldin & Katz, 2008) show that the U.S. outraced the world in education access and completion in secondary schools and in universities for most of the 20th century until about 1980. During the first period (up to 1980), inequality declined. However, the gap between those who enter and complete postsecondary education and those who enter but don't complete has been increasing over the past 30 years: "Inequality today is as high as it was during the Great Depression and probably for some time before" (Goldin & Katz, 2008, p. 3).

And this trend is not just unique to the U.S. For example, in the discussion paper for the 2008 Review of Australian Higher Education, it is noted that "the growth in university-level qualifications among the general population has not been matched by attainment of these qualifications among two of the most disadvantaged groups in Australia: Indigenous people and people from low socio-economic status (SES) backgrounds" (Department of Education, Employment and Workplace Relations [DEEWR], 2008a, p. 27). The review highlights that increasing both access and retention of disadvantaged groups in higher education is crucial not only in terms of the benefits it brings to the individuals but also to building a prosperous and socially inclusive society. The final report of the review, known as the Bradley Report (Department of Education, Employment and Workplace Relations, 2008b), makes wide-ranging recommendations which include the establishment of a national independent regulatory body; new indicators and instruments to measure and assure standards; the introduction of a voucher-based "demand driven entitlement system"; and a wide range of funding recommendations. However, of particular interest to us is the review's focus on improving low SES participation and completion rates with key recommendations being that the Australian Government set a national target of at least 40 per cent of 25- to 34-year-olds having attained a qualification at bachelor level or above by 2020. (DEEWR 2008b, Recommendation 2, p. 20) and that the Australian Government set a national target that, by 2020, 20 per cent of higher education enrolments at undergraduate level are people from low socio-economic status backgrounds. (DEEWR 2008b, Recommendation 4, p. 45).

So, college participation rates—a function of access—are still problematic, but far more important are those (typically from disadvantaged groups) who fail to complete their degrees after they enter the program: "College *completion* rates have not kept pace and the United

States has fallen to the middle-of-the-pack among OECD nations in four-year college graduation rates for recent cohorts" (Goldin & Katz, 2008, p. 326, emphasis in original). It is significant that the Gates Foundation has just retooled its strategy to include a focus on postsecondary graduation in which the foundation notes that only 20% of African American and Hispanic students who enroll in a postsecondary program actually complete their degrees (Cech, 2008; Robelen, 2008).

In summary, it is time that universities moved away from the weak metric of access (quantity) to the more revealing measure of degree completion (quality). The real economy of investment for society is producing high-quality graduates—anything less is wasteful. Whether one argues from an economic or from a moral perspective it is clear that the quality of higher education experiences and outcomes for students, especially disadvantaged ones, is declining and has been for some time. The interplay of the financial with the moral has created a core dilemma for many university leaders: how best to balance catering to market forces (and, as a consequence, achieving sustained financial viability) with delivering their mission of achieving their traditional moral and public purposes (see also Blackmore & Sachs, 2000).

Our book is about reversing the 30-year-old trend of declining quality, especially with respect to learning and outcomes for disadvantaged students. We will argue that turnaround leadership is not just about balancing a complex portfolio. It is, in a very real and multifaceted sense, about leaders fostering change-capable cultures. It is about modeling change leadership, being a learner, and giving students experiences that develop their leadership capabilities so that they enter the world of work and citizenry ready to challenge and respond to other leaders. It is about individual and societal fulfillment through the productive interplay of partisan differences leading toward greater unification of direction. Many universities, as we will show in Chapter 2, are not yet ready for this demanding challenge. But, as we will take up in subsequent chapters, it is a leadership role well suited to their greatest aspirations.

2

Failed Strategies

We start with an informal treatment of university cultures, then consider these cultures more formally. We conclude that in their present state many institutions of higher education are "change averse"; however, the hopeful news is that more and more leaders recognize the problem and want to do something about it.

Are we in the tent or out of it? In this chapter we are more outside. We think higher education has failed to live up to its own aspirations. But we also know universities well enough to recognize that many of the required elements for success exist within the institutions. It is time to forge and develop a core focus on leadership for the changes we identify in the turnaround agenda. But first, a discouraging reality.

Informal Treatment

If you spend any time in universities, or even if you observe them for brief periods of time, you will see a culture that has tendencies to be:

- Hyperrational
- Prone to talk
- Individualistic
- Dominated by research

Not all universities are like this, and universities moving in new directions is the point of this book. Some universities and their leaders are indeed well down the turnaround track. But too many, for too long, have had a culture that we would describe as "ready, ready, ready" (as distinct from our own preferred metaphor of "ready, fire, aim").

With respect to universities being hyperrational and prone to talk, for any small or big issue of the day you might say that there is an elephant in the room—and it is so damned articulate. On some days it seems that anything is worth an argument. We don't know of any study that has calculated the amount of time spent in meetings in universities, but it must be staggering. For many, university talk is simultaneously expensive and cheap (if it leads to little action). In many ways, university professors are paid to be articulate orally and in writing, and this can be both their strength and weakness. Left unfettered, academic debates generate more than their share of articulate pettifoggers and vicious politics. Harold Wilson, when he resigned as prime minister of England, was asked if he would work in a university. He responded, "No, I couldn't stand the politics."

Incidentally, for us the importance of these observations is not just that unimportant matters are sometimes debated at length but also that quite often *nothing happens*; that is, implementation is weak. Articulation in the service of clear thought and sound judgment can produce magnificent results, but this seems to be the exception rather than the rule.

Being smart and articulate is not necessarily a good thing. Pfeffer and Sutton (2000) identify the limitations of talk in the first of five barriers to closing the knowing-doing gap which they label "when talk substitutes for action":

> One of the main barriers to turning knowledge into action is the tendency to treat *talking* about something as equivalent to actually *doing* something about it. Plan-

ning for the future [is not] enough to produce the future.
[p. 29, italics in original]

Further, there are many places

> where planning activities, holding meetings to discuss
> problems and their solutions, and preparing written
> reports are mistaken for actually accomplishing some-
> thing. Such firms produce actions: meetings, conversa-
> tions, and the generation of reports. They just don't
> produce actions that have much effect on implementing
> what the firm knows. [p. 35]

Were Pfeffer and Sutton thinking about universities when they
said "appearing smart is mostly accomplished by sounding smart;
being confident, articulate, eloquent, and filled with information
and ideas; and having a good vocabulary" (p. 43)? And as we shall
argue in Chapter 3 on the new agenda, critical analysis untested
through critical doing is not even good critical analysis. In a section titled "Negative People Seem Smarter," Pfeffer and Sutton note
that "one of the best ways of sounding smart is to be critical of others' ideas" (p. 45).

We are not against good critique but against abstract discussion
that leads nowhere. In a second book, Pfeffer and Sutton (2006)
claim that in many organizations there is too much emphasis on
strategy and planning, which diverts attention away "from solving
fundamental problems and instead focuses on the intellectually
more engaging and analytically tractable issue of strategy" (p. 147).
To be both accurate and effective, critique must be pursued through
action, not through endless debates.

Relative to the third characteristic, despite traditions of collegiality and collective debates, universities are amazingly individualistic. In many ways, the incentive system and the culture reward

individualism. Except for junior professors and the growing number of part-time and fixed-term contract teachers, individual university professors have enormous freedom in what and how they teach, and how they spend their time. Scholarship by and large rewards individual contribution. Collegial interaction often masks a high degree of day-to-day individualism, and collegial talk within meetings doesn't mean anything if not much happens between meetings.

Finally, research dominates everything else to the detriment of teaching and learning, community engagement, and service. We are obviously not against scholarship. As others have observed, research disproportionately dominates the university scene whether in research-intense universities or in the aspirations of the wannabe higher education institutions who can never quite get there (Newman, Couturier, & Scurry, 2004). The answer, given the powerful competing external demands, can never be cast in zero-sum terms (for example, more research means less emphasis on teaching and service) but must be found in the synergy generated by a new way of defining and approaching the solution, which we will get to in subsequent chapters.

Formal Treatment

In some ways our informal treatment is unfair to the diversity of cultures in universities. Although the tendencies in the previous section are true, it is time to correct this incomplete depiction by introducing Bergquist and Pawlak's *Engaging the Six Cultures of the Academy* (2008). The reader will see that all of our four informal elements appear across the six cultures.

In their first edition, *The Four Cultures of the Academy* (1992), Bergquist and Pawlak identified four basic cultures: collegial, managerial, developmental, and advocacy. In their second edition, they added two: the virtual culture and the tangible culture. (It is interesting that they do not refer directly to individualism which we think cuts across all six of their cultures.) In their words: "The collegial culture [is one] that finds meaning primarily in the disciplines represented by the faculty in the institutions; that values faculty research and the quasi-political governance processes of faculty; that holds assumptions about the dominance of rationality in the institution" (p. 15).

The subthemes of the collegial culture include a disciplinary orientation, research and scholarship focus ("usually at the expense of teaching", p. 29), and faculty autonomy. Research is king in such universities dominated by powerful academic disciplines. Given the new external demands, Bergquist and Pawlak conclude: "Faculty members in a collegial culture face a formidable task: how to judge the effectiveness, let alone worth, of subtle and complex endeavors such as basic research, service to other people, and in particular, classroom teaching" (p. 41). Despite its strengths, such as deliberation and open communication, "the collegial culture suffers from a lack of organization and coherence" (p. 73). Contrived collegiality and the consensus culture are often used as weapons against change.

Second, and partly as a response to the external nonaccountability of the collegial culture, is the managerial culture: "A culture that finds meaning primarily in the organization, implementation, and evaluation of work that is directed toward specified goals and purposes; that values fiscal responsibility and effective supervisory skills" (p. 43). Here we see more pronounced expressions of "leadership and authority," a greater emphasis on "teaching and learning," and a move toward "large-scale efficiency." Managerial cultures are not good at controlling collegial cultures. In the managerial culture, there is less focus on teaching as "attention shifts from quality to workload" (p. 56). A managerial community college can become more teaching-oriented "not because it wants to be but because its faculty members have not time to do anything but teach" (p. 57).

There are still meetings galore, but in managerial cultures instead of providing an opportunity to display clever articulation, "irrelevance and inefficiency seem to pervade committee meetings." And "senate hearings are viewed with disdain. These are the 'games' that grown faculty members must play. . . to 'delude themselves' about the amount of influence they really exert on the life and goals of the college and university" (p. 69). In the new bottom line in the managerial culture, "the search for truth in higher education institutions is rivaled by a search for revenues and entrepreneurship" (p. 69).

Then there is the developmental culture: "A culture that finds meaning primarily in the creation of programs and activities furthering the personal and professional growth of all members . . . that values personal openness and service to others as well as systematic institutional research and curricular planning" (p. 73). Now we see an emphasis on faculty development, curriculum development, and long-term institutional planning. Bergquist and Pawlak identify three main features of developmental cultures: a focus on "teaching and learning" rather than traditional research and scholarship; "personal and organization maturation" through reflection and learning-by-doing; and an "institutional mission" which constantly asks, "What are we really doing in this college and university, and is it what we should be doing?" (p. 106).

The developmental culture sits uneasily alongside the previous two cultures. All that emphasis on relationships and feelings seems to be a waste of time when the answers can be arrived at more quickly through rational assessment and deliberation. Instead of being left to pursue one's own work and to show up now and then for inconsequential meetings (beyond the personal satisfaction of the most verbose), developmental cultures require too much interaction and interdependence. Managerialists don't like its indirect methods of development and idealistic pursuits.

If development is too slow, it is time to become more aggressive through the advocacy culture, "a culture that finds meaning primarily in the establishment of equitable and egalitarian policies and procedures for the distribution of resources and benefits of the institution; that values confrontation and fair bargaining among constituencies, primarily management and faculty or staff" (p. 111). The collegiality culture lacks focus, the managerial culture tries to run things from above, and the developmental culture is too slow. Hence, the advocacy culture's goals is to move things along or at least to get things right.

The advocacy culture also confronts some of the internal injustices involving the workload of junior professors and the growing number of part-time and term-limited contract teachers who are employed under conditions that, according to Gappa, Austen, and Trice (2007), can only be called "exploitative practices" (p. 96). As Bergquist and Pawlak put it: "The advocacy culture serves not only as a worthy opponent to those in the managerial culture but also as an alternative source of influence and power for faculty members who feel disenfranchised by the established collegial culture" (p. 127).

Their overall conclusion is that, while there are tensions between the developmental and advocacy cultures (the former being too soft and the latter too hard), the two agendas have much in common. Without some rapprochement between the two, "both cultures will fail to provide needed connections to the dominant and managerial cultures" (p. 129).

The fundamental problem with these first four cultures is that they all try to address the new demands of the university through internal means and perspectives—the equivalent of academic fiddling while Rome burns. The fifth and sixth cultures, while not our solution, do have the benefit of widening the scenario to simultaneously include the outside and the inside, and grounding the university more concretely.

The virtual culture is one that "finds meaning by answering the knowledge generation and disseminating capacity of the postmodern world; that values the global perspective of open, shared, responsive educational systems" (p. 147). This is the world of IT, global partnerships, and virtual learning anywhere, anytime. It is important to acknowledge this culture, but it is not at all clear what its implications are. (Our own answer will focus the solution on a specified conception of the role of the university and the leadership therein that will be required.)

The sixth culture is clearly an antidote to too much virtualism. The tangible culture "finds meaning in its roots, its community, and its spiritual grounding; that values the predictability of a value-based, face-to-face education in an owned physical solution" (p. 185). The tangible culture values "a beautiful campus, a rich endowment, prestigious degrees, esteemed faculty members, low acceptance ratios for students, and a hard-earned reputation" (p. 185). Again, the implications and even desirability of such a cultural emphasis is not clear for our purposes. We prefer to find meaning in something tangible linked to leadership capabilities and strategies for implementing it on a continuous basis.

Change Averse

The Spellings Commission on Higher Education in the U.S. identified negative outcomes arising from university and college cultures that fail to focus and establish strategies and mechanisms for quality implementation. The Commission found that:

- Too many secondary students were not prepared to succeed in college. Too many students were shopping blind having been denied adequate information.

- Once in college, too many students wasted time. . .engaged in remedial education. Too many students who started failed to finish a degree.

- Particularly disadvantaged were those students from low-income families and from racial and other minorities.

- There was a fundamental absence of transparency and hence a scarcity of "reliable information about cost and quality of postsecondary institutions, along with a remarkable absence of accountability mechanisms to ensure that colleges succeed in educating students." [U.S. Department of Education, 2006, cited in Massy, Graham, Short, & Zemsky, 2007, p. vii]

Our own research has identified additional change challenges within postsecondary institutions. These internal challenges include dealing with:

- Cultures which are change averse, "baronial," or which seek to "white-ant" necessary reform (white ant is when internal cultures interact to erode the foundation of the proposed reform)

- Structural, planning, review, and administrative processes which are unresponsive, unnecessarily bureaucratic, unfocused, and which do not add value

- Decision-making, accountability, funding, and reward systems which are inefficient or unaligned

- Patchiness and inconsistent quality in the delivery of core activities of learning, research, and engagement and the associated services which underpin them

- Change implementation strategies which are either unproductive or nonexistent

- Inappropriate approaches to leadership selection, development, and performance management

Our study of change leaders in higher education indicates that many of the strategies currently being used are inadequate and that the current focus, culture, and structure of many universities is change averse at a time when being able to work productively with change and implement needed reforms rapidly and effectively is critical to institutional survival, productive student outcomes, and national benefit (Scott, Coates, & Anderson, 2008). University cultures contain potential resources for leading change but not in their present form in most places.

We have found that a university's predominant culture ("the way we do things around here") can have a profoundly positive or negative effect on its capacity to engage with and implement necessary change. Aspects of a university culture considered to be barriers to effective change management were identified at a workshop of university leaders in 2003 and confirmed in the Learning Leaders study (Scott, Coates, & Anderson, 2008, pp. 137–138). They include inefficiency; poor decision making and a lack of focus; disengagement; unresponsiveness; unclear accountability and acknowledgment systems; unaligned structure and processes; unproductive planning and review processes; too little focus on implementation; poor leadership identification, focus, and support; underdeveloped quality management systems; and unclear standards.

Inefficiency

Indicators in this area include decision making which is ad hoc and reactive; a failure to set priorities, with everything seeming to be of equal importance; and an excessive amount of time being taken up with meetings, usually with no clear outcome. Some describe such places as "Christmas tree" universities where every day there is a new change on the agenda, with yesterday's priorities no longer of interest.

Poor Decision Making and a Lack of Focus

Indicators of ineffective decision making include more emphasis being given to "consensus around the table" than "consensus around the data"; being reactive rather than proactive; being more informed by anecdote than evidence; and giving far more focus to the present than the future and to internal day-to-day issues than external ones.

Indicators of a lack of focus include staff reporting that they are unclear on what counts most or how their work plays an important role in ensuring the university operates successfully; finding it hard to answer questions like "How do you know what is working well and what most needs improvement?"; and, when tracking data are provided, little evidence of people actively using it to set their priorities for improvement action.

A final indicator is a tendency to use a "shotgun" approach to communication. This entails sending out large numbers of e-mails and memos with no indication of the relative importance of their contents and, when there is a request for information, little acknowledgement of how what has been provided has been used.

Disengagement from the Core Purposes of the Institution

Disengagement has a number of dimensions, with key indicators including the existence of pockets of excellence which are unknown to others; a tendency for the institution to operate either as a "dark warehouse" or as a "cottage industry"; a senior executive that is not in regular contact with line staff about key issues; an intolerance of diversity or dissent; and a tendency towards group think. Other indicators include high levels of micropolitical behavior, back stabbing, passive resistance, anomic, back-room deals, little shared moral purpose, and small cliques of people being in the know whilst others feel completely left out of the action. In some cases, there is also active white-anting of change efforts, widespread cynicism, continuous leaks of negative information to the press, and a high staff turnover rate.

Unresponsiveness

Here the indicators include individual and institutional defensiveness about criticism or poor performance; an unwillingness to question traditional approaches, structures, and systems; and a tendency to transfer responsibility to others by saying "Why don't they?" rather than "Why don't we?" This is often accompanied by a heavy reliance on rigid rules-based bureaucratic procedures. Other indicators are students reporting that their queries or complaints are left unattended or are mishandled and that staff say things like "That's not my job," "It's on the Web," or "Go to another campus." This can sometimes be accompanied by staff pointing out that they are overworked and can't do any more than they are already doing.

Unclear Accountability and Acknowledgment Systems

The indicators here are staff consistently working around but not confronting poor performers; an unwillingness to raise unpleasant issues in the interests of social affinity; a failure to allocate clear accountabilities and hold staff responsible for their delivery; the existence of funding, performance management, development, and reward systems which are unaligned with key areas for quality improvement or strategic change; and limited public acknowledgment of staff who are contributing positively to the core activities of the institution.

Unaligned Structure and Processes

There are indications that the way in which some universities approach quality assurance and improvement, as well as strategic planning and review, may be unsuited to keeping them aligned with a highly changeable operating environment. There are clear connections here between the way universities are structured, their processes and preferred ways of operating, and the cultural issues just identified.

It is not always evident how support and administrative systems underpin the delivery and improvement of current programs or new developments in the core activities of the university. A good example would be moving to an online or mixed mode of course delivery with flexible attendance times without first making sure that the hardware and software, along with capable staff, timetabling systems, and library and student support services necessary to assure its delivery are in place.

More generally, the management and decision-making structure of the institution can be a powerful support for or constraint on responsiveness, engagement, and implementation. In some institutions, a very devolved operating structure is in place. This may enhance local responsiveness but can, especially when combined with revenue center management and local accountability for budget, lead to intensive, "baronial" politics and internal competition between university departments. On the other hand, a more centralized, top-down approach may maintain more control and coherence in direction but can decrease local responsiveness and staff engagement with key change projects. There are also hybrid models in which a decentralized academic operating core coexists with a more centralized system for managing the institution's administrative, HR, support, finance functions, and infrastructure. In these cases, an us versus them mentality can develop in which administrative and academic staff rarely collaborate and often work in parallel.

Another angle on the misalignment problem is the failure of individual position descriptions, performance plans, accountability, and reward and staff development systems to focus on the capabilities and priorities for effective role delivery, the quality of day-to-day delivery in research and teaching, and the implementation of key quality improvements. A need to make sure that the position descriptions for different roles are complementary has also emerged. Further, the model of learning adopted by many staff development units is often very traditional (single workshops run by people with no specific understanding of the world of the participants) and generally unaligned with helping those who are to implement necessary changes learn how best to make them work.

Unproductive Planning and Review Processes

In terms of planning, we have found that many universities currently adopt a linear rather than a cyclical, action-oriented, or embedded approach to planning. This modal approach puts the most energy into writing the plan and launching it rather than into making sure it is monitored and implemented consistently, effectively, and sustainably.

The many current approaches to strategic planning tend not to be sufficiently evidence-based or informed by comprehensive tracking data and strategic intelligence. In such cases, planning and decision making, as noted earlier, tend to focus more on consensus around the table rather than consensus around the data. Plans tend to be produced in glossy form, launched at a large function, and then forgotten—with little tracking of their implementation or accountability for failure to deliver on the key targets and changes they contain. The motto, as we noted earlier, often seems to be "Ready, aim, aim, aim," "Let's set up a subcommittee," or "Let's have another review" rather integrating planning with action and, through this, learning how best to make a desired change work by doing it under controlled conditions, refining it, and then scaling it up. Associated with this is a tendency not to productively involve the people who are going to have to implement it.

Similar problems emerge with the way in which many universities approach reviews. These tend not to be embedded or ongoing and are often undertaken on a fixed cycle, irrespective of need or risk, every three to five years. Furthermore, they often look at departments, faculties, or units in isolation from those other parts of the university with which they must work in collaboration to be effective. In the worst cases, the review creates large amounts of work in gathering out-of-date, unbenchmarked data for an external panel which adds little value by suggesting improvements, pointing out what everyone already knew, or making recommendations based on what has already passed.

So, at present there is limited practical understanding in many institutions that change is a cyclical and ongoing process, not a linear one, and the implementation of the associated cycle of planning, action, review, and improvement in universities now sought in external higher education quality audits in many countries remains patchy.

Too Little Focus on Implementation

As just indicated, the tendency in many universities is to invest most of their effort into developing plans, running retreats, undertaking reviews, and identifying what should happen with far fewer resources being put into making sure that what emerges is consistently and effectively put into practice. There are links here to a continuing preference in many universities to focus on inputs and resources allocated as a measure of quality rather than outcomes and impact. Furthermore, there is evidence that some current approaches to implementation may be making things worse and that the use of external consultants to lead change may not be cost-effective.

Poor Leadership Identification, Focus, and Support

We have found that leaders—both central and local—encounter considerable frustration in trying to deal with arcane systems and a change-resistant culture as they work to engage and support people in necessary change. Yet we have also found that there is often little attention paid to the capabilities and experience necessary to lead change in the position descriptions for leadership roles in higher education. Furthermore, the sorts of support which university leaders identify as being most productive in developing their capabilities and performance as leaders is only rarely promoted by university staff development units. Finally, effective and systematic approaches to identifying and developing potential leaders is neglected, despite the leadership succession crisis which is now upon universities as the large cohort of Baby Boomers moves toward retirement.

Underdeveloped Quality Management Systems

Given the pressures exerted by the external forces outlined in Chapter 1, especially the need to ensure that our institutions of higher education not only gain but retain students, over the past decade there has been increased interest in quality management—in finding out what works best to both assure quality and improve the total student experience of the college or university. The particular focus of these developments has been on determining how best to ensure consistency and equivalence of quality within and between universities and across locations. However, we have found dramatically different levels of development of efficient and productive quality management systems between universities in the same country and between countries.

In some countries where external quality audit systems have been introduced across the entire higher education sector, much more systematic attention to quality management has emerged. In some cases, there are national quality tracking systems for learning and teaching as well as for research. In most countries, however, the approaches to quality management are more idiosyncratic. Thus it is impossible for individual institutions to systematically and conveniently use comparative data to identify key areas for improvement, find proven solutions in other locations, or establish areas where they are doing well compared with similar universities elsewhere.

Where such systems are operating well, there is still a tendency to produce quality reports with much less consistency in ensuring that the key recommendations for improvement that they contain are addressed promptly and wisely. In addition, there remain the challenges of ensuring that what is tracked is valid and distinguishing between the use of the data generated for formative as distinct from summative purposes. A parallel problem is seen in the inadequate way in which the outcomes of internal tracking reports and reviews are often followed up.

Unclear Standards and the New Focus on Outcomes

There is a general shift across many higher education systems to a focus on outcomes rather than on inputs as key measures of quality. There is particular interest in determining how a university can show it has added value to student capabilities and has done so at a university standard. However, the sophistication, reliability, and validity of the measures used appear to be variable.

Our study of more than a quarter of a million "best aspect" and "needs improvement" comments written by graduates in 14 Australian universities on their total university experience (Scott, 2006) shows that the lowest odds of a best aspect comment is in the area of assessment of learning—in particular in its relevance, marking, expectations management, and feedback.

As Derek Bok (2006) put it: "Although the attacks on college professors seem clearly overblown, there is a subtler problem with faculty behavior. . .However much professors care about their teaching, nothing forces them or their academic leaders to go beyond normal conscientiousness in fulfilling their classroom duties. There is no compelling necessity to re-examine familiar forms of instruction and experiment with new pedagogic methods in an effort to help students accomplish more" (cited in Massy, Graham, Short, & Zemsky, 2007, p. 6).

Conclusions

So far we have painted a somewhat dismal picture. But for all their hyperrationality and academic cultures, institutions of higher education can accomplish impressive breakthroughs when they put their minds and hearts to work on focused problems. Liker and Meier (2007), in their detailed analysis of Toyota culture, quote Edgar Schein: "Never start with the idea of changing culture. Always start with the issue the organization faces; only when those . . .issues are clear should you ask yourself whether the culture aids or hinders resolving the issues. Always think of the culture as your source of strength. It is the residue of your past success" (Schein, 1999, p. 189).

Many a president or dean has been run out of town for tackling directly the cultures of the academy. Instead, our message is start with the issue(s) the organization faces, refocus the agenda, use the considerable extant change knowledge, and then shape and leverage the strength of existing cultures and their leaders. In Chapter 3, we get to the actual change agenda and how to pursue it. The agenda is a synergizing, coherence-making proposition. Society is badly in need of new leaders who know how to reconcile divisions. Universities have a major role to play in modeling how divisive problems can be better tackled and in producing graduates who can be leaders who can address complex problems of the day. The beauty is that the change agenda is an integrating one, and thus core leadership practices can meet many needs simultaneously and cohesively.

If the challenges from within the universities are addressed along the lines we suggest in the next three chapters, we have clear evidence that the institutions concerned will be far better positioned to negotiate successfully the challenges posed by both the external and internal environment. And they will be better able to model how differences can be constructively reconciled to achieve productive change and to produce the new generation of change leaders so desperately needed in the current context.

3

The New Agenda

With all the cross-cutting demands upon them, universities and colleges need a small number of "integrators" that best address the idea of the university and equally "how" to pursue this idea. We think this is best achieved by focusing on (1) practical reasoning—a more integrated conception of the role of knowledge that combines collaborative engagement with real-world issues, analysis, and application; (2) putting teaching and learning at the center of the traditional triumvirate of research, teaching, and university engagement and service; (3) turning inquiry on itself to establish quality processes, data, and implementation; and (4) building the corresponding leadership capacity based on theory and knowledge. This is the new agenda with all four elements intimately interconnected including the specific capabilities and capacities required for leading learning. These developments are entirely consistent with turnaround leadership and indeed serve to clarify and deepen the focus on change-capable cultures.

Practical Reasoning: Combining Analysis and Application

The secret to universities fulfilling their mission involves recasting how knowledge is conceived. Specifically, critical analysis must be refined in the crucible of doing, and action must be assessed in terms of its underlying theory of cause and effect. Done well, this meets several goals simultaneously: it produces better knowledge and theories; it satisfies and prepares students better; it results in better teaching; and it serves the needs of communities more powerfully, neither ignoring nor pandering to them. In brief, it produces the kinds of citizens and leaders we need for reconciling fractious organizations and societies.

A particularly well-developed version of this new agenda, complete with detailed premises and examples in liberal arts and the professions, is contained in Sullivan and Rosin's *A New Agenda for Higher Education: Shaping a Life of the Mind for Practice* (2008). Sullivan and Rosin (2008) set out to examine "how the liberal arts and the professions might serve one another, in ways that are more symbiotic than oppositional" (p. x). The authors start with the question of whether university students could become good citizens "if their liberal learning were solely theoretical" (p. xi). Their answer is a resounding no, and instead they set out the limitations of the analytical process of conceptualization, addressing the dilemmas of practice and theory if each is uninformed by the other.

Sullivan and Rosin's new understanding of the purpose and outcome of higher education has dramatic implications for the role of knowledge and teaching: "The academy is not only called upon to break apart the world into its constitutive relations and causes through critical thinking. . .we mistake analyses and critical thinking, which are disintegrating ends, for judgment and responsibility, which are integrating and consummating ends. . .Our students will be called to take up concrete places and stances in the lives of others. They must learn to discern the practical salience of academic insight through integrative acts of responsible judgment in the world. What critical thinking pulls apart responsible judgment must reconnect" (p. 143).

In any argument, critical thinking by itself fuels the divide on both the left and the right, when what we need is thinking, judgment, and action that understands, tests, and reconciles differences,

all within a clear moral purpose. The core purpose of higher education is, therefore, not to impart knowledge or develop people who
are only good at analysis or critical thinking. It is, rather, in the
words of Sullivan and Rosin, "to prepare students for lives of significance and responsibility [by developing] a life of the mind *for
practice* (p. xv, italics in original). This life of the mind for practice
means developing students' capacity "to blend knowledge, skill, and
appropriate attitude in response to unique situations that require
expert judgment" (p. xxi).

Sullivan and Rosin capture how this approach works in practice
in their developmental seminars with professors teaching in this
manner in the following domains: (1) human biology, a course
which "engages students in serious consideration of some of the difficult intersections between biological science, morality, and social
policy" (p. 5); (2) ethical issues in engineering, a course in which
"students explore a particular documented event that raises difficult
questions about the ethical nature of engineering practice" (p. 10);
and (3) contracts, a course for first-year law students which helps
distance students from their "misguided sense of the certainty of the
law's application" (p. 16). Students are taught to think through specific applications and dilemmas taking into account the social
meaning of context in order "to weigh two divergent contexts: (1)
consistency of application, and (2) equity or justice of outcome" (p.
19). Sullivan and Rosin furnish several other course examples:
"issues in Jewish ethics," "ethics and law in medicine," "foundations
of modern education," "engineering cultures," "advanced legal
ethics," and "scripture and moral life." In a word, the entire university is implicated in this new work.

The common thread to this new integration is teaching "practical reason" which helps students "move back and forth between
the general theory typical of their fields and the demand to make
their learning and intentions concrete in particular judgments and
decisions" (p. 19). In other words, there is much more to university
education than critical thinking. By itself, critical thinking is bad

theory because it fails to grasp the meaning and required action in specific situations. And it unwittingly furthers divisiveness, or at least leaves it unreconciled. Practical reasoning is not antithetical to the traditions of universities. In fact, it underpins much of their efforts in applied and engaged research. The point is that it must be brought forward and recast as a central integrator in the new agenda of universities and colleges. We could not agree more with Sullivan and Rosin's major premise that "higher education [needs to] provide formative experiences that enable students to gain orientation in the world, acquire the intellectual skills necessary for engaging their world, and develop reflective and ethical commitments in response. . .[These courses] teach the art of practical reasoning— the art of placing analytical concepts into a mutually illuminating relation with sources of meaning and responsibility in the world of practice" (pp. 22–23).

Sternberg and Grigorenko's (2003) triarchic theory of intelligence fits well here. They identify three components:

1. Analytic intelligence: the ability to complete academic problem-solving tasks such as those used in traditional intelligence tests.

2. Creative or synthetic intelligence: the ability to successfully deal with new and unusual situations by drawing on existing knowledge and skills.

3. Practical intelligence: the ability to adapt to everyday life by drawing on existing knowledge and skills in deciding what needs to be done [p. 10].

Of course, Sullivan and Rosin's point is teaching these competencies in an integrated fashion—something not being done in most universities today.

Sullivan and Rosin's agenda also mirrors Henry Mintzberg's (2004) devastating critique (and corresponding solution) to the teaching of MBA students. Sullivan and Rosin's following observation about practical assessing could be inserted on almost any page in Mintzberg's book without skipping a beat: "Practical reasoning and valid higher education experience is about participation and engagement with real-world problems and perplexities, not the abstract dissection associated with critical thinking and traditional university analysis" (Sullivan and Rosin, 2008, p. 10).

Mintzberg (2004) argues forcefully that analysis without action is sterile: "Strategy is an interactive process, not a two-step sequence; it requires continual feedback between thought and action. Put differently, successful strategies are not immaculately conceived; they evolve from experience" (p. 55). This contrasts with the university's tendency to engage in analysis, meetings, talk—ready, ready, ready—instead of applied learning through action. Similarly, Duggan (2007) claims that the reigning strategy paradigm misses the point: "It tells you how to analyze your own strategy. . .but it does not tell you how to come up with a strategic idea" (p. 3). Effective ideas emerge through reflective action. This is not just about doing; it is about how to obtain valid conceptual insight. Universities must turn their attention to teaching students how best to gain conceptual insight as they grapple with applied problems. Universities then need to develop strategists—graduates good at strategizing or moving back and forth between thought and action—not analysts. Strategy is not strategizing.

Khurana (2007), in his careful history of business schools in the U.S., *From Higher Aims to Hired Hands*, draws essentially the same conclusion: "Institutions charged with educating and developing professionals (or leaders for that matter) need to actively shape professional identity—that is how one conceives of oneself and one's relationship to work. For professions, at their core involve a complex sense of identity rooted not only in expert knowledge. . .but also in commitment to a set of collectively held norms" (p. 371).

There is no clearer instance of the issues we have been discussing or opportunity for turnaround than the leading role which higher education can play in helping us address the issues of climate change and environmental sustainability. In the U.S., for example, the Obama-Biden Environment and Climate Change Plan has profoundly important implications for the turnaround agenda of the country's universities and colleges. Many of the plan's initiatives will require these institutions to take on a leadership role, to undertake research in partnership with their communities, government, and industry, and to produce graduates with the commitment and practical reason to enact it. It is an agenda that is not only about technology and invention but is also about figuring out how best to engage everyone in day-to-day change at home, in the community, and in the workplace.

This dual focus is clearly seen in the Obama-Biden plan. It includes increased investment in basic research, venture, and human capital for clean energy; sets an objective to have 25% of U.S. electricity come from renewable resources by 2025; and requires all new federal buildings to have zero emissions by 2025 (with all other new buildings to be carbon neutral or have zero emissions by 2030). It gives high priority to achieving energy conservation; allocates significant investment in advanced vehicle technology, mass transport projects, and new fuel-efficient cars; and proposes a range of clean water and water conservation initiatives. It also aims to provide the American people with the necessary tools to achieve these targets; to give greater attention to technology transfer; and to establish a Clean Energy Corps to assist with implementation.

The core role of universities and colleges for turnaround in this area has multiple dimensions. All of the following options were identified at the Association for the Advancement of Sustainability in Higher Education (http://www.aashe.org/) conference in 2008:
Universities can:

- Act as living laboratories which model to students and their communities what going green looks like

- Study and help us understand the key issues—like the interface between rapid population growth in developing countries, a "growth fetish" (Hamilton, 2003) in the developing ones, the scientific facts of climate change, how to change human behavior—and help us invent the solutions to the predicament the world now finds itself in

- Reduce their own emissions by ensuring that both their new buildings are LEEDS compliant and that existing ones are retrofitted to make them more efficient

- Use their students as agents for behavior change within and beyond the institution

- Institute green purchasing policies

- Conserve water and recycle all waste

- Use their buildings and facilities all week and all year round, not just during weekdays and two major semesters per annum

- Look at more efficient forms of travel, timetetabling, and learning

- Give concerted focus to both researching and studying key issues of social, economic, and environmental sustainability in every course they teach.

Lester R. Brown (2008) outlines the overall dimensions to be addressed in his book *Plan B 3.0: Mobilizing to Save Civilization*, and Rappaport and Creighton (2007) in their book *Degrees That Matter: Climate Change and the University* draw out some of the specific implications for action by universities including buildings and facilities; saving energy; purchasing; transportation; dealing with waste; engaging staff; action in the classroom; and taking an interdisciplinary approach to the study of climate change in the curriculum.

As Sullivan and Rosin (2008) suggest, the complex issues raised above are not just for the professions. The humanistic tradition of liberal arts and the sciences "is deeply committed to the development of students' capacities for the critical interrogation of experience. . .As such, the humanistic and professional domains have much to learn from one another" (p. 115). The liberal arts and sciences critical analysis tradition potentially has much to offer the professions. These disciplines could furnish the critical lens for understanding the broader social, historical, and contextual forces faced by professionals in everyday life and the dilemmas they generate. Yet: "These experiences, which ought to provide students with a sophisticated understanding of the contexts and institutions of their future action, occur typically in the moments farthest removed from the everyday world. Moreover, liberal education is usually pursued in a fashion that is unresponsive to the problem of meaning and the diverse practices that populate society" (Sullivan & Rosin, 2008, p. 91).

All of this has substantial implications for universities to move toward more transdisciplinary programs that reconnect critical analysis with engagement in society and culture in "an integrated vision of higher education that is insightful liberally, informed scientifically, and responsive practically" (Sullivan & Rosin, p. 136). This is clearly a vision that challenges the current structure, funding, cultures, and management systems of universities. Addressing the new vision is not as impossible as it might seem. Our change theory provides guidelines for thinking-doing-learning that link building ownership and skill. In a sense, universities need to practice this on themselves in order to learn how to teach it. Teaching and learning practices and organizational life are closely connected.

The preceding claims by Sullivan and Rosin (2008) and others are congruent with our own and colleagues' studies of effective professionals (Schön, 1983), successful graduates in nine professions (Vescio, 2005), skilled Olympians (Scott & Saunders, 1995), effective school principals (Scott, 2003), and, as we shall see later, higher education leaders (Scott, Coates, & Anderson, 2008). In this work, which we call "the professional capabilities framework," the goals are:

1. To identify the capabilities that are most important for successful professional practice in the first years after graduation

2. To determine the extent to which the universities have focused on developing these capabilities

3. To review existing curriculum and assessment in light of the findings in items 1 and 2

We will take up the details of the findings in subsequent chapters, but in essence the framework for professional capability includes and integrates four (a later iteration identifies five) components: emotional intelligence, ways of thinking (diagnostic maps), profession-specific knowledge and skills, and generic knowledge and skills. These are the interlocked sets of competencies and capabilities rated as most important by successful graduates for effective early career professional or disciplinary practice. They are also the skills least likely taught in an integrated way in most university courses.

We like Francis Bacon's metaphor: "We rise to great heights by a winding staircase." Effective approaches to helping students develop their capability to undertake the circuit of practical reasoning and for proceeding up the winding staircase of capacity development requires: engagement with concrete practice in the discipline or profession; experiencing a perplexity and the need to act in a situation; making sense of this using diagnostic maps developed through reflection on earlier similar but never identical experiences; having to read the situation in order to figure out what is going on; formulating what seems to be a uniquely suitable response; and testing this response in the situation, evaluating the results, and adjusting one's strategy accordingly (see Scott, 1999). And, as we shall see in Chapter 4, this is precisely how effective universities negotiate the volatile environment in which they now find themselves.

Practical reasoning is reasoning *from* cases not *to* cases. This is a critical point about sequence and consistent with our theories of action derived from education systems (Fullan, 2008b) and with the findings from effective businesses (Fullan, 2008a). Well-analyzed new experience precedes insight; behavioral change feeds into change in belief. There is a role for theory, but it "emerges properly *through* the consideration of practice, rather than the other way around" (Sullivan & Rosin, 2008, p. 70, italics in original).

Spohn (2003), one of Sullivan and Rosin's colleagues, states the main point succinctly: "We are more likely to act ourselves into new ways of thinking than think ourselves into new ways of acting" (p. 13). As Kurt Lewin (1945) put it more than sixty years ago, "There is nothing so practical as good theory." And we would add, as David Hunt (1987) has said: "There is nothing so theoretical as good practice."

Far from abandoning the intellectual traditions of the university, practical reasoning actually *strengthens* them. Critical thinking by itself, observe Sullivan and Rosin, "is a vague and often poorly conceived notion of educational purpose, more like a slogan than well-formed educational ideal" (p. 95). Thus, practical reasoning develops better clarity of thought. Teaching critical thinking does not, in other words, develop more effective critical thinking applied to real problems. Practical reasoning addresses the university's main intellectual purposes on its own terms. It results in *better knowledge*.

In a similar vein, O'Meara and Rice (2005) outline Ernest Boyer's (1990) influential work in *Scholarship Reconsidered* and the ways in which his ideas have been addressed in U.S. higher education over the past two decades. Of particular interest to us is Boyer's conception of the scholarship of integration and how this relates to the other, more familiar forms of scholarship—the scholarships of teaching and learning, discovery, and engagement.

Boyer's conception of the scholarship of integration concerns making connections across the disciplines and placing them in a larger context. This aspect of the Boyer agenda, along with a focus on learner-centered teaching and two-way engagement, has much in common with our focus and Sullivan and Rosin's (2008) concentration on practical reasoning through engaged learning and research with key issues of social, economic, and environmental sustainability, as they affect both the professions and the disciplines. Boyer's agenda aligns with our view that a new, more integrated conception for learning and teaching is central to the future of the academy over the coming decade. But note that, so far, the integration component of Boyer's agenda of almost 20 years ago has only been acted upon in a patchy way. The good news is that through Sullivan and Rosin (2008), we have a sharper picture of what it looks like in practice. And our ability to link it to leadership and the change-capable culture (Chapters 4 through 6) makes it all the more powerful.

We know that the approaches identified by Sullivan and Rosin (2008) have been used in individual classrooms for decades and that problem-based learning has been the focus of some university programs for a long time. However, what we are advocating is that Sullivan and Rosin's (2008) focus on practical reasoning and Boyer's (1990) focus on the scholarship of integration now be pursued with consistent, strategic intent *across the whole university*. There are turn-around universities where this is now happening. A good example is Arizona State University (ASU):

> The key to (ASU President) Crow's vision is to break away from the department model of most universities, and instead build up excellence at problem-focused, interdisciplinary research centers. U.S. research universities, Crow argues, "are at a fork in the road: do you replicate what exists, or do you design what you actually need?" By his reckoning, centers that teach students to communicate with the public to tackle real problems, such as water supply, are more relevant to today's needs than, say, a chemistry department. . . . All of this is part

of an overall picture that puts strong precedence on three things: high quality, interdisciplinary research; access for large numbers of students from Phoenix's racially and socially diverse population; and relevance to the needs of the city and the region. . . . But the entire project undoubtedly hangs on Crow's unique style of leadership. The approach is unusual, as Rhodes (former president of Cornell University) notes, because presidents of US universities often have to content themselves with refining what they have already got. "The polishing of the status quo is much more comfortable," he says. [Macilwain, 2007, pp. 968–970]

Arizona State University then states, "The successful ASU graduate is a change agent, equipped with the knowledge, ability, and desire to lead and change the world" (ASU, 2008, p. 7).

On the other hand, we need to be careful not to get carried away with this change agentry stuff. Stanley Fish (2008), a law professor and former dean of arts and science, argues forcefully that university professors and their students should mind their own business and that their business is *only analytic*. We agree partially with Fish when he says that university people should not meddle outside of their own areas of expertise and that they should not get carried away with the political emotions of the day. If you read our claim carefully, it is not about advocacy but rather about immersing oneself in applied as well as analytic reasoning. We are in favor of greater expertise in which theory and practice are integrated, where applied practice contributes as much to better theory as the reverse. We beat Fish on his own terms in that academic knowledge is all the stronger because of reasoned, applied practice. And by the way, our approach will address the current appallingly low completion rate of 40% of students graduating from four-year programs. So, be careful, but be there.

In short, the new core agenda for postsecondary institutions is knowledge-based practical reasoning and judgment which can help to reconcile differences in a divided society in order to reach new levels of individual and societal fulfillment. This goal is not foreign to universities but is vastly underrepresented. We believe it must become the preeminent goal of universities and colleges. However, three other related developments must accompany practical reasoning if it is to become reality.

Teaching and Learning at the Center

There are many reasons why teaching and learning must become the integrator in the traditional university triumvirate of research, teaching, and service and engagement. If knowledge-based integration of the three components is the goal, it is far more effective to build this integration around teaching and learning than to start with either research or service. Trying to do all three independent of each other is a recipe for fragmentation and failure. Research has the natural upper hand. Teaching and community engagement and service, if attempted in silo fashion, will always be mediocre.

We often talk in elementary and secondary schools about the privatization of teaching. Universities are, if anything, worse: "Teaching remains too often a private practice performed by sole academic proprietors, rather than a public and scholarly practice through which insight is developed progressively over time" (Sullivan & Rosin, 2008, pp. 128–129).

The importance of this new centrality of teaching and learning is that it will engage students in productive learning, retain them to degree completion, and result in better graduates (and, we daresay, will generate better research, community engagement, and service overall). We explored the student perspective on quality learning in our CEQuery analysis of 280,000 comments made by 94,000 graduates from 14 Australian universities about the best aspects of their experience at university and those which most need improvement (Scott, 2006).

The results of the CEQuery analysis have been benchmarked and refined against the findings of parallel work in the U.S. (Swail, 2006; Kuh, Kinzie, Schuh, & Whitt, 2005; Pascarella & Terenzini, 2005). The findings have then been critically appraised and validated in a series of national workshops undertaken with more than 400 leaders and researchers across Australia in 2005 and 2006, along with international workshops and discussions with over 500 leaders and researchers across South Africa, New Zealand, and Canada over the same time frame (Scott, 2006). What has emerged is a set of principles or quality assurance checkpoints for ensuring that universities not only gain but retain students and engage them in productive learning. The key findings are as follows.

It is the Total Experience That Shapes Productive Learning, Not Just What Happens in the Traditional University Classroom

> *The challenges concerning student engagement involve much more than academics—it's about the overall higher education experience students encounter on a day-to-day basis, from the moment they set foot on campus to commencement (if they get that far). Facing the challenges concerning student engagement requires a keen understanding about remediation issues, retention rates and the expectations of a diverse student population (adults, Millennials, NetGeners and everyone in between); providing timely and efficient student services; getting faculty to modernize from a technology perspective; and making meaningful lifelong learning connections. [Segall & Freedman, 2007, p. 4]*

Students' judgments of quality can be shaped just as much by what happens as they enroll, the quality of their encounters with academic and administrative staff, the quality of learning resources they can access, and their overall sense of being supported by and belonging to an institution as by the quality of the teachers and their classroom learning experiences. In the U.S. the NASPA (2004 and 2007) *Learning Reconsidered* publications explore this issue in detail.

They recommend that courses be designed in a way that takes into account the broader university experience—not just the academic context but core elements of the social and institutional context like enrollment processes, course advice, support for students at risk, peer support, campus life, library resources, IT facilities, and so on (NASPA, 2004, pp. 14–15). Equally, this implies that what is tracked during implementation must cover the total experience, not just what happens in the traditional classroom.

Learning Is a Profoundly Social Experience

As Gay and Hembrooke (2004) conclude: "Learning is built up through conversations between persons or among groups and involves the creation of shared understanding through social interactions" (p. 32).

The quality and net effect of encounters with both academic and support staff, along with the extent to which one becomes part of a supportive peer group, have a strong impact on student focus, persistence, and retention. This implies that how students form positive networks needs to be more directly considered, using the best aspects on this subdomain from the CEQuery analysis as one source of ideas. It also implies that all staff need to be alerted to the importance of being positive and responsive in their encounters with students.

Learning Is Not Teaching

> *A paradigm shift is taking hold in American higher education. In its briefest form, the paradigm that has governed our colleges is this: A college is an institution that exists to provide instruction. Subtly but profoundly we are shifting to a new paradigm: A college is an institution that exists to produce learning. This*

shift changes everything. It is both needed and wanted.
[Barr & Tagg, 1995, p. 1, emphasis in original]

It is critical that the terms *learning* and *teaching* are not conflated. Teaching is what teachers do, learning is what students do. A wide range of learning methods were identified in the CEQuery study (Scott, 2006) as a best aspect of students' experience of university. These are summarized in Table 3.1. There are two observations to make about the findings.

First, traditional teaching methods (like lectures) do attract some best aspect comments. However, as Table 3.1 shows, by far the highest proportion of best aspect comments are about active learning, not teaching, experiences in which students work on problems, construct understanding, and develop relevant knowledge, skills, and ways of thinking. The high-rated learning methods are extensive. They range from face-to-face activities including group projects, discussions, and debates; to a wide range of real-world, practice-oriented learning experiences; various forms of independent study; learning via simulations; and the active use of IT in multiple ways to find, shape, and share information, not simply to passively read it.

Second, considerable disciplinary bias was found in the best aspect learning methods identified. For example, in the health and education fields, almost all of the best aspect comments were associated with clinical placements, and practical and experiential learning. On the other hand, in the commerce and business areas, case-based learning was most popular (incidentally it also attracted a larger number of needs improvement comments, indicating that its effective use is inconsistent). This finding suggests that there may be considerable opportunity to explore the use of the highest rated learning methods in one field of education in another where they are little used.

These results highlight the importance of academics in turnaround universities becoming much more effective at learning design rather than continuing to impart information via the traditional lecture. To be clear, we are not arguing that we should remove lectures. Rather we need to give lectures their right role as part of a much

Table 3.1. CEQuery best aspect learning methods sorted by type

Face-to-Face	Practice-Oriented and Real-World	Independent Study	Simulations and Labs	CIT-Supported Learning Methods
Lecture (interactive)	Clinical placement	Learning by completing assignments/essays	Mock trial	Online search for information/Web sites
Group project, small-group work	Practicum, practical teaching,	Writing a research or community service report	Role play	
Tutorial	Teaching rounds		Simulated interview	Web-based learning—WebCT, Moodle, Blackboard, etc.
Class-work exercises	Practical legal training	Use of self-teaching/distance education packages	Educational game	
Discussion, sharing ideas	Cooperative education		Discovery learning	Blogs, MySpace, Facebook, etc.
Seminar/individual presentation	Work experience or placement for work-based learning	Self-teaching guide	Experiments	
Workshop	Supervised practice	Project report writing	Lab work	Online study
Debate	Professional mentor	Proposal writing	In tray exercises	E-mail contact with staff/students
1:1 consultation	Learning by doing	Learning contract	Use of a simulator	
Mentor (peer or staff)	Field study, work experience, site visit			SMS with staff/students
Conference/symposium	Camps			Individual phone contact with staff/students
Forum/panel				
Exhibition				

(Continued)

Table 3.1. CEQuery best aspect learning methods sorted by type (Continued)

Face-to-Face	Practice-Oriented and Real-World	CIT-Supported Learning Methods
Peer learning and support	Addressing real-life problems	Teleconference, YouTube
Group dynamics exercises	Guest speakers, industry/professional representatives	Teletutorial
Critique of student production/creation	Practical work at university	Video conference
Buzz group	Design studio	Podcasts/MP3
	Artistic production	Radio
	Placement or study overseas, or in another local university	Audiotapes, CDs
	Real-life case study	TV
	Applying learning to work problems	Video/DVD
		Photos, slides, digital images

more comprehensive, student focused, distributed, and active learning system. Traditional lectures work best when they inspire, set a context and framework around the learning to follow, recap and clarify how elements of the course fit together, drive home key points, and so on. Lectures are much less engaging and productive when they are used to simply impart information (see Bligh, 2000).

Multiple Methods for Learning

The CEQuery research found that what works best is the right combination of the active learning methods identified in Table 3.1, not just one or two. In doing this, universities should, as Sullivan and Rosin (2008) advocate, be giving emphasis to active, integrated inquiry and action-based learning around real-world issues and dilemmas rather than concentrating on passive learning of content in a disaggregated set of subjects and lectures. As noted, one can find pockets of such an approach in some universities, but for most this would require a major cultural change (Scott, 2006).

A Focus on Assessment of Learning

What emerges very clearly is how poorly managed assessment design and delivery continue to be. The Spellings Commission recommendations and related accountability pressures have led to a focus on standardized measures of student outcomes and assessment which, in turn, has resulted in institutions seizing upon instruments that may not be valid or at all integrated with processes for improving teaching. As Ewell (2007) puts it: "One disturbing aspect of the post-Spellings world is an unprecedented level of rhetoric around instruments" (p. 14).

The CEQuery research confirms that it is assessment (what assignments students have to do, how they will be graded, what is in their exams, whether there are clinical and practical placements that will be evaluated, and so on) that drives learning and that students tend to look first at what has to be produced to get through a course before they look at other aspects of their subject outline. They look to see if what is required for assessment is relevant and engaging; that the way in which they are to be graded is clear; and then to how all of the learning methods and resources identified in their subject outline might help them complete these assessment tasks efficiently and effectively. They repeatedly call for more timely and constructive feedback on their assessment tasks, for examples of good practice on how to do assignments at the subject level, and for clearer expectation management, more consistent marking, and better coordination between subjects to ensure that assessment deadlines are staged so that not all assessment tasks across subjects are due at the same time (Scott, 2006).

Assuring the quality of learning assessment and standards is, as noted in Chapter 1, of increasing importance. In this regard, there needs to be explicit attention paid to its validity—in particular to ensuring that what is assessed focuses on the capabilities essential to successful disciplinary and professional practice along the lines identified by Sullivan and Rosin (2008), as well as the key graduate attributes set down in each university's mission. Equally, the quality of the assessment tasks themselves must be assured. Integrated, problem-based assessment items are much more telling than those that require simple factual recall of course content. Finally, grading must be demonstrably at a university standard, focused on assessing higher order capabilities, and students must be clear from the outset how their work will be evaluated.

Addressing such issues is a critical quality assurance issue for higher education in the current context, not only because it is assessment more than anything which drives learning in our universities but also because valid and reliable assessment determines the quality of our graduates and assures our standards. Moreover, meaningful assessment influences student motivation and continuous learning in the short run and in the pursuit of graduate studies in the longer term.

Self-Managed Learning

A key finding from our research on student engagement and retention is that students respond best to a self-teaching guide for each subject which

- Outlines the assessment tasks to be produced

- Says why each task is relevant to successful professional or disciplinary performance

- Shows the links between this and other subjects

And then makes clear

- How grading will occur (with annotated examples)

- When and how feedback will be given

- How the full range of learning experiences and resources designed into the subject can best be used to complete each assessment component

This focus first on outcomes and then how to achieve them addresses a recurring needs improvement finding in the CEQuery research that learning designs which are more input and content oriented, rather than assessment and outcome oriented, are confusing and unengaging (Scott, 2006).

Multiple Designs for Learning

The CEQuery research indicates that a one size fits all approach will neither engage students in productive learning nor retain them. We must be more responsive and able to read (diagnose) what is likely to engage each new group of students by looking at their particular backgrounds, abilities, needs, and experiences and then to match a learning design with the right combination of learning methods (Table 3.1), attendance patterns, assessment strategies, content, and learning materials that best fit this diagnosis, keeping in mind the capabilities necessary for effective subsequent professional or disciplinary performance and available resources (Scott, 2006). It is in this way that the flexibility, relevance, and responsiveness identified by graduates in the CEQuery analysis as a best aspect of their university experience can be more consistently achieved. This finding also calls into question the drive in some contexts to opt for cost-efficiency by seeking to modularize the curriculum into a set of content-focused learning packages and putting it all online (Scott, 2006).

All of these findings clearly have major implications for how faculty teach and how they learn how to teach more effectively. Turning around universities means that improving faculty teaching must become a core purpose—for the good of their students' learning and for the good of their scholarship.

Faculty Development

Since the new agenda calls for new pedagogical approaches to student formation and learning design, it follows that there is a major challenge involving corresponding faculty formation or development. The context for some of this work (with one major qualification) is well set out in Gappa, Austin, and Trice's (2007) *Rethinking Faculty Work*. (The qualification to which we will return later is that Gappa et al.'s treatment is faculty-centric; that is, it fails to explicitly connect faculty formation to the new agenda of student formation). The lack of an explicit link notwithstanding, Gappa et al. (2007) have set the context correctly. Their purpose is to investigate these questions:

- What enhances the ability of academic institutions to recruit and retain highly capable faculty members?
- What are the essential elements of academic work and workplaces that will help ensure faculty find their work satisfying and meaningful?
- How can colleges and universities fully recognize and build on the intellectual capital that faculty represent, and on the talents and abilities of each member of the faculty? [p. xii]

The reader will note that students are conspicuously absent from the list. The assumption that students will be better off if faculty are engaged more meaningfully is too implicit.

Nonetheless, Gappa et al. (2007) depict the current problematic situation quite well. Fiscal constraints and increased competition, calls for accountability, growing enrollment and increasing diversity of students, and the rise of the information age combine to de-center the traditional university. (This, incidentally, is why we call for a small number of focused components to act as integrators for the new agenda.)

Faculty composition itself is radically changing. In the U.S. in 1970, 80% of faculty were full-time tenured with 20% part-time or fixed tenure. By 2003, the proportions were 55% and 45%, respectively, with the trend increasing (Gappa et al., 2007, p. 55). Drawing on the basic research on job satisfaction, Gappa and her colleagues remind us that effectiveness requires that employees, like students, feel that their work is meaningful, have a sense of responsibility in their job, and have knowledge of the results of their work (p. 121). These findings echo our own conclusions in *The Six Secrets of Change* (Fullan, 2008a). Gappa et al. argue that current external factors (as in our Chapter 1, for example) are eroding these three psychological sources of satisfaction and effectiveness for faculty in the 21st century and will continue to do so if action is not taken to counteract them.

Gappa et al.'s (2007) own solution is to focus on five interrelated elements, namely, greater employment equity, academic freedom and autonomy, flexibility, professional growth, and collegiality. Anchored in a core of "respect," the five elements of faculty work experience are intended to result in the following five outcomes:

1. Increased faculty satisfaction and sense of meaningfulness
2. Increased organizational commitment
3. Enhanced recruitment and retention
4. Broader spectrum of individuals represented in the faculty
5. More strategic utilization of intellectual capital [p. 134]

Note that there is no link at all to a change-capable culture (our Chapters 4 to 6), nor are their recommendations explicit enough about how those outcomes could be obtained.

By and large, Gappa et al. (2007) have identified and reinforced the earlier conclusions about the growing challenges and the negative organizational consequences for universities, but much more needs to be done to figure out the turnaround leadership that would be needed to address the issues raised by Gappa and her colleagues.

Within the domain of faculty development, we would expect every university to have a center or office of teaching improvement. The jury is still out on this one as it all depends on what the office or center does. This is a necessary but not sufficient step, as such a center would be only one component in the turnaround movement we are discussing. We don't see these centers operating in a one-size-fits-all mode but rather in the spirit of practical reasoning. Such a center would have the responsibility of stimulating inquiry, development, and sharing of effective practices. We should see teaching and learning scholarship and practice being highlighted as a new core mission of the university. At a minimum it would turn the spotlight on teaching and address the basics of good teaching (in light of the fact that university professors typically have no training in pedagogy). At a maximum it would foster and be responsive to new programs and practices that represent integration of critical analysis and application through new curriculum and pedagogy. Such centers should not be content with the mere recognition and spread of good teaching. They must also get at the underlying principles of effective learning, course design, and assessment. The research we introduce later shows that academic staff like to learn how students like to learn—just in time, just for me, problem-based, with solutions from successful practitioners in their area linked to their skill gaps, and so on. The ideal way to help academics understand how to deliver what students respond best to is to have faculty experience it in their own learning.

Both of our universities have taken steps to focus on improvements in teaching. The University of Toronto, with 60,000 students, is a relative newcomer, having established an Office of Teaching Advancement (OTA) in 2002, and is about to enter its second phase (www.utoronto.ca/ota). The University of Western Sydney, like most Australian higher education institutions, has had a longer tradition of concentrating on teaching and learning and the formation of students using nationally gathered tracking data. In addition to the focus on advancing teaching, UWS has also established quality reviews, data gathering, and implementation processes as being central to the work of the university, what we have called "turning inquiry on itself". This is a crucial step because it goes beyond having a support unit for improving teaching (which is still good in its own right) to building ongoing quality improvement into the line authority, daily practice, and core operating systems and accountabilities of the university—something, as we have said, that is not traditionally a strong suit of postsecondary institutions.

Inquiry, Quality Reviews, and Implementation

We state briefly here the nature of this work because we get into the details as part of the turnaround strategies in Chapters 4 through 6. In essence, the new agenda includes institutions of higher education acting like any learning organization, which is to say that they must gather focused data on their own practices and outcomes, have mechanisms for implementing improvements, and to do this continuously and consistently, not in a pocketed fashion. In short, universities must practice what they preach and become good at applying and modeling the principles of practical reason on themselves and to their students, and at identifying and disseminating successful professional and disciplinary practice.

We have already established in Chapter 2 that only a limited number of universities engage in the systematic quality assessment of their work in teaching and learning. For research, there are built-in reviews of quality in terms of funding decisions and in peer evaluation of scholarship and publications, but this is not always the case for determining the quality of the student experience, community engagement, or service.

Massy, Graham, Short, & Zemsky (2007) identify seven myths about quality:

1. Quality depends mainly on spending

2. Research automatically improves teaching

3. Good teachers are born, not made

4. It's the best and most motivated students that matter

5. Teaching is a lone-wolf activity

6. Quality is good, absent evidence to the contrary

7. Education quality can't be measured

After countering the myths, the authors then set out seven quality principles to guide quality audits:

1. Define quality in terms of outcomes

2. Focus on how things get done

3. Work collaboratively

4. Base decisions on evidence

5. Strive for coherence

6. Learn from best practice

7. Make continuous improvement a priority

Massy et al. (2007) stress that the main goal of quality reviews is not external accountability but rather to help departments and faculty improve the quality of their work. The authors then furnish templates, guidelines, and several concrete examples of quality reviews being documented in named institutions. These audits, conducted well, can be an excellent lever for achieving internal improvement and culture change.

It is important to note that local quality audits are different from the traditional external program reviews that are conducted in most universities at the end of a decanal or departmental chair term. Local quality audits operate best when they are built into the internal running of the university and are solely for internal improvement. They require going beyond establishing centers for the improvement of teaching by creating quality assurance units in the office of the provost or vice chancellor.

One final note, one we make in all of our change work. A quality audit is only a *tool,* and a tool is only as good as the mindset using it. There are no shortcuts to improvement. There must be a clear and widely held conceptual mindset that underpins quality reviews—one that cultivates clarity about the content of the new agenda and the action assumptions that guide how to get there. This takes up the fourth and final component of the new agenda.

Change Theory and Leadership

If you are going to have a hope of changing an institution with eons of history, you have to tap into some aspects of existing culture. Abrahamson (2004) talks about "change without pain" (actually change with less pain than usual). He argues that some organizations, when faced with relentless external challenges, make the mistake of engaging in what he calls the repetitive change syndrome. The result is a combination of initiative overload, change-related chaos, and employee burnout and cynicism.

Instead, Abrahamson calls for "creative recombination" in which institutions draw on and integrate existing strengths that reside in their "corporate basement"—a process that consists of "finding, reusing, redeploying and recombining mismatched parts that the organization already has" (p. 10). If you examine closely Bergquist and Pawlak's (2008) academic cultures and our new agenda, you will discern that for institutions of higher education this means integrating, in particular, the collegial, developmental, and advocacy cultures of the academy. This is not an easy integration—such is the mastery of leading change in higher education in the 21st century.

The key design criteria here are coherence and motivation. In other words, what conceptions and strategies will provide clarity and consistency in a way that results in motivating critical masses of people to obtain positive outcomes for students and the institution on a continuous basis? We have had success in doing this in the public school system in Ontario with its two million students and 4,900 schools by basing our theory of action policies and strategies on combining the following six elements: direction and engagement, capacity building with a focus on results, supportive infrastructure and leadership, managing the distracters, continuous evaluation and inquiry, and two-way communication (Fullan, 2008b). And we will show later in this book that the same lessons apply to universities.

Direction involves leaders having a good conception of the new agenda while engaging organization members in its pursuit. It requires equal measures of conviction and connection around this agenda. Capacity building pertains to the development of the key knowledge and capabilities required in relation to outcomes. Infrastructure and leadership consist of establishing and developing leaders at all levels of the organization skilled at collectively engaging in the new agenda. Managing the distracters is addressing issues that divert energy from tending to the small number of new core goals. And two-way communication means, on the one hand, continually conveying the goals and means of the new agenda, and, on the other hand, listening to the feedback in order to make adjustments and refinements as you proceed. This is not abstract theorizing. All of it is based on applied change strategies that get results. Further, it applies for all; everyone needs to become a leader in their own area of expertise.

We will identify the specific change leadership qualities in Chapter 5. For now we stress that these qualities concern the ability to empathize, that is, capture the reality of divergent groups, in order to lead a process of change which reconciles differences, thereby motivating previously divided individuals and groups to become more unified on a higher plan of development. This is something that great leaders have always been adept at in times of societal upheaval including Lincoln, Mandela, and, apparently (we shall see), Obama.

This change capability is not just for great leaders. All university leaders must cultivate it in themselves and in their students. Then we will see great change that has sustainability through continuous reconciliation and continuous learning.

To do all this is going to require systematic leadership in all quarters of the university. Postsecondary institutions are going to have to do something that they have never done. Instead of appointing the smartest people in the room to leadership posts (or, in the case of departmental heads, enlisting whomever's turn it is, in which case they may or may not be smart), higher education institutions, like any of the top organizations in the world, *will have to deliberately cultivate leadership capabilities within their own ranks*. Turnaround must be brilliantly and sensitively led. The latter is the focus of the remainder of this book.

4

Making It Happen
Building Quality and Capacity

Failed implementation is the bane of all change aspirations.

In Chapter 1, we argued that a compelling combination of extrinsic and local change forces are bearing down upon our universities. In Chapter 2, we concluded that our higher education institutions need to become more change-capable if they are to successfully negotiate these forces. We noted in particular that our universities often spend too much time discussing what should change and too little time figuring out how to make desired changes happen. As we have argued, good ideas with no ideas on how to implement them are wasted ideas. In Chapter 3, we presented a new higher education agenda, an outline of *what* needs to be done for higher education institutions to serve and position their countries in the new environment. In this chapter, we look at the empirical research on the *how* of effective change management and implementation in universities, at how universities might become more change-capable and, through this, implement the new agenda which we have proposed.

First, we emphasize that context counts. For example, the culture of the university or college (how we do things around here) needs to enable it to constructively, collaboratively, and productively negotiate the highly volatile operating environment it now faces. At the same time, the institution's structure and operating systems need to be agile, supportive, and efficient. This is important because it gives university staff room to change, learn, and lead.

Second, we emphasize that people count. For example, if the staff and leadership of an institution do not have the capabilities to effectively implement change, then necessary change efforts will stall.

Whereas Chapter 2 identified failed strategies, this chapter identifies successful ones. We profile a change-capable university culture, note how closely this will align with the profile of the change-capable university leader identified in Chapter 5, and how it models for students what responsible judgment, practical reason, and reflective action (Chapter 3) look like in the daily practice of a learning organization.

We distinguish between the key concepts of quality improvement and strategic positioning; identify what constitutes an agile and efficient structure of decision making and operating systems; and show how an effective higher education institution, like an effective higher education research team, operates on evidence, not on anecdote. We then look at how the focus in our universities needs to shift from strategic planning to strategic thinking and doing and how, exactly, the process of continuous quality improvement can operate in both our core activities of teaching, research, and engagement, as well as in the many support systems that underpin them.

Finally, we look at how to optimize the engagement of those people who will ultimately be the ones to implement changes like those identified in Chapter 3, the line academics and general staff who work each day with our students.

Some of the key messages that will emerge are that:

- Change is a complex learning (and unlearning) process for everyone concerned. It is not a one-time event.

- Context counts. An overly bureaucratic operating system, a relentless round of meetings with no outcome, staff who are unresponsive or uninterested can all prevent a desired change from working in practice.

- We need to operate on evidence, not on anecdote.

- Our focus needs to be on determining the quality of results, that is, the quality of outcomes and impact, not just the quality of inputs.

- The more we can be proactive rather than reactive the better.

- As we shall see in Chapter 5, change does not just happen; it must be deftly led by people who understand and base their actions on the above lessons.

At the end of the last chapter, we identified six key elements that characterize a change-capable educational institution: direction and engagement, capacity building with a focus on results, supportive infrastructure and leadership, managing the distracters, continuous evaluation, inquiry, and two-way communication. This chapter shows how these elements can be implemented. And it shows how the optimum culture creatively combines the most productive aspects of the collegial, developmental, managerial, advocacy, virtual, and tangible cultures discussed in Chapter 2.

A Change-Capable University Culture

The distinguishing aspects of a change-averse culture were outlined in Chapter 2. The Australian Learning and Teaching Council leaders and reviewers identify how to produce a more change-capable culture (Scott, Coates, & Anderson, 2008). They provide an operational picture of the attributes of an effective learning organization and show how the six key elements of effective change management can be realized.

Change-capable universities:

- Are *undefensive*. When faced with an unexpected event, a crisis, negative feedback, or a disappointing performance, the institution and its leaders accept that this is inevitable and are neither defensive nor panicked. Rather, the institutional response is calm, the uncertainty is tolerated, and there is no personal blame. Everyone simply tries to figure out collectively what might be causing the problem and how best to respond to the situation in a measured way.

- Are *evidence-based*. Like their best teams of researchers, change-capable universities figure out what is going on and how best to respond based on evidence, not anecdote.

- Set *priorities*. The institution and its leaders set a small number of relevant, feasible, and widely understood priorities for action.

- Can make a *hard decision*. They do this in a transparent, evidential manner, after taking input from all concerned on what might be the most relevant, desirable, and feasible way to respond.

- Make *clear who is responsible* for what activities, how different roles complement each other, and hold those who occupy them accountable for the outcomes of their efforts.

- Acknowledge that *all staff* have a role to play in supporting successful delivery and change, not just academic staff but administrative and general staff as well.

- Are *outcomes focused*. That is, they not only seek to assure the quality of inputs (such as plans, courses, projects, and resourcing), but they also track the quality of their implementation and, most important, the quality of their impact on those intended to benefit from their work.

- Ensure that *complex, hierarchical approval systems* are only used when justified—for example, when there are key risks to be managed. When this is not the case, decision making and sign-off are given to locally accountable staff for quick response against a common set of guidelines. At the same time, they ensure that when hierarchical approval processes are used they demonstrably add value and are not simply ritualistic.

- Make sure that all *meetings* are justified, cost-effective, fit for purpose, and expertly chaired, with a focus on ensuring that they are outcomes focused, with clear follow-up and accountability for delivering on the actions agreed.

- Operate in a *responsive, collaborative*, team-based, and focused fashion.

- Learn how to make their agreed strategic developments and quality improvements work by *trialing them under controlled conditions*. That is, they seek, whenever possible, to shape, test, evaluate, and refine desired changes in a controlled environment before scaling them up.

- Are *strategically networked*. They work closely with like institutions elsewhere in order to benchmark, identify improvement solutions, and generate strategic intelligence on forthcoming developments that will affect them.

As noted earlier, this institutional profile closely aligns with the distinguishing capabilities of the most effective leaders of change in universities (Chapter 5). It also has close resonance with the key capabilities required of our graduates in the current context, for example their capability to engage in practical reason (Chapter 3) and the distinguishing attributes identified in research on successful graduates (Vescio, 2005).

Using a Quality Audit to Build a Change-Capable Culture

External and internal quality audits can be used as a lever to shift the culture and operating systems of a university toward the change-capable profile outlined above (see Scott & Hawke, 2003, on how external quality audits have been successfully used and Massy, Graham, Short, & Zemsky, 2007 on the productive use of internal audits).

The focus of an external quality audit is typically on many of the attributes of a change-capable university just outlined. For example, such audits seek to confirm if the institution is consistently achieving its mission and objectives to a satisfactory standard; that it is taking an evidence-based approach to decision making; and that it is not only tracking the quality of what is being delivered but is also promptly, wisely, and consistently addressing the key areas for improvement which emerge from this process.

Once staff know that the audit will be focusing on such issues, recognize that the report on the audit is to be made public, and see the consequences of a negative audit in other universities, there is a considerable increase in their extrinsic motivation to address recurring areas of poor practice and adopt the attributes of the more change-capable culture identified. At the same time, if the whole process is handled well—by focusing on the moral purpose of the university, the personal benefits of decreasing unnecessary bureaucracy, developing a more systematic approach, and increasing the university's focus on what counts—we have found that staff become intrinsically motivated as well.

An Agile and Efficient Operation

One of the key tasks in building a change-capable university is to manage the distracters. In Chapter 2 we identified a number of these. They include meetings which are neither fit for purpose nor have a demonstrable outcome; unnecessary travel to such meetings; inefficient administration; overly complicated and slow sign-off systems which do not add value; and unproductive micropolitics which cause more time spent on intergroup positioning and denigration than working on how best to deliver the optimum experience to students.

Yet there are universities where each of these distracters has become the focus of considered action; where unnecessary meetings have been discontinued; where simple teleconferences have been substituted for travel to face-to-face meetings; where chairs are trained on how to run a productive meeting; where alternative, less time-consuming ways of gathering views have been considered; where clear agendas and advanced preparation and focus are put in place to make the meetings that are held cost-effective; and where participants are not all sitting around engaging in the "Blackberry prayer" (the tendency for people at an unengaging meeting to bow their heads checking and sending e-mails under the table).

Operating on Evidence, Not Anecdote

As noted above, a key component of a change-ready culture is to ensure that decisions are evidence-based. Such a focus should rest comfortably with academics, as it is the central foundation for their scholarship. For example, no researcher, peer review panel, or doctoral supervisor would accept a research report, conclusion, or thesis based on anecdote. Thus, "managing the nature and quality of student learning outcomes, maintaining continuous improvement and providing a consistent flow of evidence are all vitally important when developing successful institutional strategies. . . Accrediting agencies create clear expectations for institutions and programs to 'define, collect, interpret and use evidence of student learning outcomes'" (Segall & Freedman, 2007, pp. 5–6; see also Pfeffer & Sutton, 2006).

Yet, as noted in Chapter 2, a focus on robust evidence is often not front and center when it comes to making decisions about what most requires improvement and attention in universities, what their key strategic directions should be, or how well their core activities are currently working in practice. Turnaround universities acknowledge the importance of the consensus culture. However, they shift the focus from consensus around the table to consensus around the data. A university culture characterized by a commitment to continuous evaluation, inquiry, and quality improvement concentrates on using evidence to identify what aspects of its current provision are working well and what most need enhancement. Here the focus is on the present. However, the other side of the change coin involves keeping an eye on the future. This involves figuring out against the available evidence the optimum direction for the university and determining what is the most relevant, desirable, and feasible way to make sure it is positioned sustainably into the future. Whereas quality improvement focuses on making sure existing provision is working well, strategic positioning focuses on making sure the university remains in alignment with a rapidly changing external environment. Each of these key elements of a change-capable university is discussed below in more operational detail.

Effective Approaches to Quality Tracking and Improvement

It is critically important that an IT-enabled tracking system is put in place which enables the university not only to monitor its performance but also to track the extent to which its key strategic developments and quality improvements are working in practice by, for example, checking if they are attracting consistently high levels of user satisfaction, retention, and impact.

There are indications that, when such systems are in place, considerable improvements in overall student engagement, satisfaction with their university experience, and retention can be achieved. This is because the university is able to determine where to focus its improvement energies, what to concentrate on, and if the implementation of these key changes is proving to be effective. In the University of Western Sydney, for example, we saw an improvement of 10% in student satisfaction over three years and an improved retention rate of 4% over the same period (Scott, Grebennikov, Shah, & Singh, 2008). A significant explanation for this was the fact that the tracking systems for the first time made clear where improvement efforts needed to be directed and what exactly needed improvement.

An example of an effective university tracking and improvement system for learning and teaching is outlined below. It received a commendation in the university's external quality audit in 2006. The system is nested; that is, it brings together satisfaction survey results and outcome data at four levels:

- Students' feedback on their total university experience from teaching, facilities, support, and the library, to student associations and infrastructure. This survey is undertaken every two years.

- Program-level performance including benchmarked trend data on demand, retention, progression, completion, graduation rates, employability, and salaries as well as satisfaction data from a national course experience questionnaire and a qualitative analysis of open-ended comments on that questionnaire. Reports at this level are produced annually.

- Unit (subject) feedback data on 13 key items known to be of highest importance to student retention. Benchmarked reports at this level are produced every semester.

- Feedback on teaching data. These are produced and returned with benchmarked results to the teachers concerned and considered in staff performance reviews.

In addition to the above core tracking tools, additional surveys are undertaken. These include a first-year exit and retention survey and an employer survey. The university also has an online complaints management system. This identifies programs, services, and aspects of practice attracting repeated complaints. Those responsible are assisted to address the causes of these complaints, thereby avoiding having to repeatedly treat the symptoms.

Whenever possible time series, benchmarked reports are delivered, typically within a month of the data being gathered. At the same time, diagnostic reports which consolidate and triangulate the findings from the individual surveys and outcome data are produced centrally in a form and at a time requested by those who are to address the results. The system is enabled by a set of data cubes with custom-tailored extraction programs designed to meet user needs for specific tracking reports.

The tracking and diagnostic reports produced by this system are used to both prove and improve the quality of learning and teaching and are linked to both the establishment of key improvement priorities at the department, school, college, and university levels, as well as to performance and improvement funding rewards. The university's Learning and Teaching Action Plan is directly informed by the consolidated analysis of all of the data produced by this tracking system. For example, current key priorities for improvement include targeted transition assistance, creating a more flexible and responsive learning environment, and improving assessment quality and feedback.

Careful attention is given to ensuring that the items in all these surveys are valid. Two strategies are used to ensure this is the case. In key surveys, students are invited to rate not only the performance but the importance of each area surveyed. In addition, items are those which attract the highest number of hits in the qualitative analysis using the CEQuery tool of some 280,000 best aspect and needs improvement comments written on the national Higher Education Course Experience Questionnaire (Scott, 2006).

The areas consistently attracting the highest importance ratings in the quantitative and qualitative data produced by the system are used not only to track what is happening but also to assure the quality of course design. Those areas attracting high importance and low performance ratings become key priorities for quality improvement action. This saves considerable time and resources by making sure that effort is not put into trying to improve areas that are relatively unimportant for productive student engagement and retention.

The university uses the national course experience survey to enable it to identify areas attracting high performance ratings in other universities where its own ratings for the same area are lower. This process of benchmarking for improvement is reciprocal. That is, universities sharing data agree to offer improvement solutions to each other.

Shifting the Focus from Strategic Planning to Strategic Thinking and Doing

Strategy formation, as we said in Chapter 2, is one of the least understood aspects of change management in higher education. Yet, in the challenging operating environment currently faced by universities, concentrating solely on monitoring and improving current provision in the ways outlined above is highly risky. Being change savvy is crucial. In addition to the theory of action ideas at the end of the last chapter, we offer the following more operational elements.

Decisions about where a university is to head and how it is to be structured must be evidence-based. As noted earlier, such a proposition should not be new to academics. It is also at the core of what any learning organization is about. As Ramaley and Holland (2005) note: "The role of the academic leader in this model (of change management in universities) is identical to the principal investigator in any research project" (p. 81).

Being evidence-based and results-oriented in setting its strategic development priorities requires the university to draw upon not only existing performance and trend data but also on strategic intelligence gathered through research, targeted networking, and benchmarking with institutions that have similar missions, both locally and overseas. Sources of evidence include feedback from employers and the professions, from successful graduates, disciplinary networks, government officials, and policy advisers, along with close analysis of national and local social, economic, environmental, and technological trend data.

Accessing and including the student voice as a source of evidence is a particularly important element in this process. However, it cannot be assumed that elected student representatives will accurately represent the full range of views of their constituency. Their input should be supplemented by a consolidated analysis of quantitative and qualitative student feedback provided through the university's tracking and improvement system, along with consulting successful graduates and using focus groups on key issues.

Consistency with mission, relevance, distinctiveness, and feasibility are the key tests as this evidence is scrutinized to identify the key areas for strategic action. In so doing, a focus on strategic thinking rather than strategic plans is necessary. In this regard, a useful analogy is to see the university as a fleet of ships. Strategic thinking is about figuring out where the fleet might best head without spending too much time on producing detailed advanced plans on what will be done day to day to get there. This recognizes that how each ship and the fleet makes its way toward the agreed destination depends on negotiating daily the changing, often unpredictable, sea of forces. As Ramaley and Holland (2005) observed when discussing their experience with institutional change at Portland State University, "change can set in motion reactions that ripple out in unpredictable and unanticipated directions. Thoughtful and well-grounded adjustments in strategy are often needed to accommodate these reactions and unintended consequences" (p. 78). The art, then, is to know where the institution is collectively heading but not to stick too rigidly to a preset course. In this way the repeatedly noted propensity in higher education to endlessly plan and review without seeing any real movement in daily practice can be reduced.

All of this implies that it is important for the university to set just a small number of evidence-based key strategic directions to pursue, directions which both internal tracking data and external strategic intelligence suggest to be the most relevant, desirable, distinctive, potentially productive, and achievable. There will always be far more change possibilities and directions to take than there is the time or capacity to implement.

Adopt a Ready, Fire, Aim Approach

To work, shifting the focus to strategic thinking requires a considerable change in culture. To survive and thrive in the uncertain context of the 21st century, universities have to shift from a propensity to engage in ready, ready, ready (have a subcommittee conduct a review, etc.) to ready, fire, aim—a process in which ready is a need to act, fire is to try out a potentially viable response under controlled conditions, and aim is to articulate what works best and scale this up once it has been tested and refined. Having an effective tracking and improvement system like that outlined earlier is essential to enable the trial process of potentially viable change solutions and refining them to be evidence-based and informed before scaling up.

Steering Through Engagement

Lillis (2007) concludes that the most effective model involves what she calls "steering through engagement," in which top-down and bottom-up approaches are used together.

There is consensus in the literature that, to be effective, strategic planning has to engage with the academic heartland and, therefore, the extent of a consultative process is a major factor in process design in higher education [p. 30]. . . . The comprehensive departmental and institutional review ensures that institutional goals are set on an informed basis. This is a considerably stronger starting point than the standard strategic planning model which depends primarily on a one-off environmental analysis. It also tempers the level of ambition that rational strategic planning permits and ensures that the constraints of the operating environment are considered from the outset. Self-study on its own is open to the challenge if all change is incremental and a projection from the current state of affairs where no major changes are possible. The "steering by engagement" model takes the incremental changes proposed by the self-study and provides an opportunity to compare them with the challenges faced by the Institution [p. 33].

In this combined top-down and bottom-up approach, a small set of carefully formulated and nonnegotiable parameters for change are set as a result of linked institutional and local review against a comprehensive set of evidence (both on current performance and predicted changes in the institution's operating environment). Then local units, led by accountable senior staff, are invited to determine through self-assessment, benchmarking for improvement, networking, and input from a wide range of stakeholders how these directions can be best implemented, given their unique and detailed knowledge of local conditions.

Documentation captures both the outcomes of the review and the planned direction indicated by the consolidated institutional and local diagnoses of what must be done against the evidence reviewed. It is in this way that the fleet analogy discussed earlier can be operationalized. Overall direction is set by the university taking into account not only internal but external input. However, each unit runs its own ship and makes its own way toward the agreed destination, adjusting, negotiating, and learning what works best as it does so. This approach is, also as noted earlier, more about ready (we need to change, that is, move), fire (let's get under way, learning what works as we go), and aim (now we can articulate what works because we've done it). This is seen as being more productive and engaging than the more traditional ready (we need to move), aim (let's stay in the harbor having meetings about what course to take), aim (let's have a review), aim (let's discuss the review), aim (let's bring in a consultant), and so on.

This notion of ready, fire, aim aligns with the cycle of review (self-study), plan (identify a response), implement (put it into practice), monitor (check the outcomes), improve (retain what works but address what doesn't) favored in various higher education quality management and auditing systems around the world.

As Lillis summarizes it:

> The "steering by engagement" model engages with the academic heartland at three critical points. Firstly the academic heartland is involved from the outset in the initial self-studies, the outcomes of which are collated for consideration at the institutional level prior to setting institutional priorities. This provides departments with an opportunity to influence institutional goalsetting, highlight their achievements and identify problematic areas.
>
> . . . The second critical point of engagement is when academic departments are asked to develop their own plans in support of institutional priorities. Instead of being asked to implement someone else's predetermined strategies, departments have the flexibility to develop their own solutions to the challenges presented as appropriate

to their context. By comparison to a model where solutions are developed by a small group of sages at the top of the organization, this also significantly increases the chances that innovative solutions will be developed as the full capacity of the staff, through their respective departments, is being harnessed. Senior management teams can concern themselves less with the detail and concentrate on how well or otherwise the Institution's strategic objectives are being achieved.

The third point at which the academic heartland is engaged is through the development of annual Personal Development Plans which are aligned to their department's objectives. This increases relevance, ownership and maps some responsibility from the department to the individual. [p. 33]

Engaging Staff with Necessary Change

A common error is not to develop sufficient ownership of a needed change by those who are to implement it. Ownership (like learning) is best created through purposeful action, two-way communication, and engaging those who are to implement a proposed change by inviting them to help determine what is going to be most relevant, desirable, feasible, and productive, always with a focus on results. It is important to ensure that such involvement is neither contrived (here's the plan, just approve of it) nor anecdotal (let's go for consensus around the table rather than consensus around the evidence). Furthermore, formal meetings are not necessarily the best way to secure the sort of involvement and commitment necessary for staff to engage with and persevere with making a needed change work.

For example, a range of strategies, directly generated from research on what is necessary for effective change implementation in universities, have been used to engage staff at the University of

Western Sydney with the data produced by the university's tracking and improvement system.

- The system is centrally run, and consolidated reports are produced at a time and in a form that the staff identify as being most helpful and convenient.

- At the same time, overall tracking reports for the area against a set of agreed criteria are given twice a year to the university's board of trustees.

- Staff and the relevant academic leaders are asked to check the diagnostic report for their area against the data provided and then to identify the key areas for improvement they intend to pursue, along with areas of good practice which they recommend be adopted in other programs. These action plans are presented, discussed, and noted at the Education Committee of the senate which also compares results with the previous year.

- The key areas of good practice and agreed improvement priorities inform the institution's learning and teaching action plan for the coming year and are discussed at the annual quality forum. This includes all the university's senior staff as well as the heads of all programs. The same plans for improvement action identified for the Education Committee are built into each school's action plan for the area.

- A linked set of key staff are accountable for ensuring that action is taken on the results. These include a pro vice chancellor (learning and teaching) and an associate dean (learning and teaching) in each college, and teaching fellows responsible for specific universitywide improvement priorities. Their performance reviews address outcomes achieved in the quality improvement projects for which they are responsible.

- A network of heads of programs, led by the pro vice chancellor, looks at the best ways to implement the change priorities in the unique context of their local course and share-effective solutions.

- Both intrinsic and extrinsic staff motives are addressed. The senior leaders emphasize the moral purpose of what is being done, especially praising the improved retention and completion rates of students who are first in their family to attend university. At the same time, key extrinsic motivators are noted, including praise, reward, promotion, and the financial (and employment) consequences of a failure to retain students. A key additional lever for engagement is the fact that external quality audits focus specifically on the extent to which line staff are aware of tracking data and have successfully and consistently addressed its key improvement messages.

- The service philosophy of the central office of planning and quality is an additional motivator for engagement, especially since that office does most of the work in gathering, analyzing, and producing consolidated diagnostic reports for the convenience of staff.

- Students are told what is happening with their feedback via posters which are placed in prominent places across the campuses, on the university's Web-based learning system, and at their first class each semester. This has two important outcomes: first, students see that it is worthwhile giving feedback and that it is acted upon; second, the staff concerned have an increased incentive to do what they promised.

- Action on the results is led by senior college and
  school staff and is team-based, with monitoring data on
  outcomes being made available to each team as implementation proceeds. The general motto for implementation is "why don't we" not "why don't you."

A similar self-assessment approach can be taken to engage staff
with reviews and external quality audits. For example, many external audits and internal review processes start by inviting the university or unit to produce an evidence-based self-assessment. This
is an important strategy for developing ownership of the outcomes,
helps identify better improvement solutions, and assists those who
are to implement the changes that emerge to own the process.

We now have empirical evidence to confirm that this approach
is indeed more productive than the more top-down, cascaded
approach to strategic planning and change management traditionally used by universities. Lillis (2007), in a series of studies of different approaches to strategy formation, found that self-study
approaches were far more effective than traditional, top-down
strategic planning processes on the following outcome criteria:
(1) the degree to which the planned changes subsequently met their
goals; (2) whether they tackled core academic issues; (3) the percentage of outcomes that could be ascribed to the program (net outcomes); (4) whether informants perceived the programs to be
effective; and (5) other improvements arising. Massy and his colleagues (2007) corroborate the importance of self-study and its place
in effective quality review cycles.

The above strategies align with the key findings outlined in
Chapter 3 on what engages students in productive learning. These
findings confirm that what engages staff in productive change
is what engages students; that the total experience counts, not just
what happens in a formal class (or staff meeting); that learning is a
profoundly social experience and that one's peer group plays a key
role in engagement and perseverance; that people learn best by

doing and seeing positive outcomes from their efforts; that continuous evaluation, feedback, and support on how to address weak areas of performance is especially valued; that expectations must be clear; and that being able to self-manage one's learning helps.

Key Implications for Action

These ideas are consistent with our own findings on how to achieve effective change in large systems. It requires a small number of core ambitious goals implemented deeply through the blending of direction and engagement (Fullan, 2008a, 2008b).

There are four recurring change themes that underpin the discussion so far:

1. Change is a complex learning and unlearning process for all concerned. It is not a one-time event.

2. Organizational and individual capabilities to manage change are directly linked. Change-ready and -capable organizations are made up of change-ready and -capable staff.

3. Of course, there is a big difference between change and progress. The former is about something being made different or becoming different. The latter involves coming to a value judgment about the worth of each change effort. Change management is, therefore, heavily value-laden.

4. Strategic change and continuous quality improvement are two sides of the same coin. The former is concerned with setting and implementing new directions, the latter with ensuring that current practice is regularly tracked and the key areas for enhancement identified are addressed promptly and wisely.

Having good ideas for building a change-capable culture and advocating a new approach to strategic change and quality improvement will not make change happen in daily practice. Such changes don't just happen, especially in university cultures which have many autonomous and isolated parts. Leadership—ever-widening circles of leadership—is absolutely critical to grappling with the forces of change and nonchange that we have been discussing in this book. Coordinated and sustained leadership, which is not higher education's strength, will be the key issue in postsecondary institutions in the next five years. The specific quality of this leadership will literally determine which institutions survive and thrive in the context of the external and internal forces now bombarding universities.

Note, we said the *specific* qualities. What exactly characterizes quality leadership, and how do we develop it at all levels of the university? We will get to a more comprehensive framework in Chapter 5, but let us consider a more concrete example of turnaround leadership.

University of Pretoria, South Africa

From 2000–2007, in post-apartheid South Africa, Jonathan Jansen was the first black dean in an all-white university. He arrived at the parking lot gate his first day on the job and said, "Good evening comrades. I am the new dean of education; can I get my key?" The two gate attendants laughed, bending over in mirth.

"Yea, right," said one of them. "And I'm Bishop Tutu."

How do you change a 100-year-old white university? One parking space at a time. Jansen then began a seven-year struggle to change the culture of an institution embedded in the past but facing the stark reality of racial and cultural integration. Talk about turnaround!

Jansen's theory of action is remarkably congruent with our leadership capability framework. Leading culture change from a minority position in a deeply entrenched institution of more than 40,000 students and 2,000 staff on 7 campuses requires all the emotional intelligence and resilient courage that one can muster. We cannot possibly do justice to the profound cultural upheaval for both blacks and whites in those seven years; see Jansen's (in press) moving account in *Knowledge in the Blood*.

In a briefer treatment, Jansen (2008) reflects on and identifies seven theses that underpinned his theory of action and that kept him going on the most depressing days:

1. We must reorganize the politics of emotions that energize behaviors.

2. The change strategy cannot create victims.

3. The problem must be named and confronted.

4. Leaders must exemplify the expected standards of behavior.

5. We must engage emotionally with students in their world.

6. Teachers and principals themselves are emotional actors.

7. The environment must accommodate risk [p. 189].

Reminiscent of *Lincoln's Virtues* (Miller, 2002) and Mandela's quiet persistence and inclusiveness, Jansen demonstrated incredible empathy for both blacks and whites, as he simultaneously, transparently, and persistently confronted the profound personal and institutional politics and emotions.

Examine the dilemmas in the following two situations:

> In the case of the lecturer who intersperses her teaching with snide racial comments about the capabilities of black students, a leader must make it clear that racism is unacceptable, that a higher standard of behavior is required, and that the continuation of racial insult will lead to dismissal. . .The confrontation is not about the lecturer per se; it is about broader communication to the watchful audience of campus dwellers and surrounding communities for whom taking a stand is an indication of

what is acceptable and what is not; and of the position of leadership on this potentially explosive issue. [Jansen, 2008, p. 240]

At the same time, Jansen is able to empathize with

Max, a teacher of South African history. . .for more than 25 years. As a white South African reared in the political vortex of the apartheid years, Max came to understand deeply that the history of white settlement was one of triumph over adversity, of civilization over backwardness, of Calvinist faith against atheistic communism, of freedom against tyranny. He lost members of his family in the border wars, witnessed the struggle of his parents against white poverty, and then the gradual rise, through the discipline of hard work, to a comfortable though not extravagant middle-class lifestyle. Then Nelson Mandela was elected in 1994, and a new history was suddenly to be taught with a different narrative from the ones he had come to believe and thus relied upon to make his choices in life. For him, the teaching of history is emotional knowledge, even though he accepts, in his mind, the inevitability of a new official knowledge. [p. 243]

Thus, turnaround leadership involves combining direction, empathy with different groups, reconciling divisions, and displaying great courage, perseverance, and resiliency. Being tough and being emphathetic are not mutually exclusive. Balanced leadership indeed!

Note the remarkable parallel to Barack Obama's (2008) handling of the situation when his black pastor, Jeremiah Wright, denounced on videotape America's racism, "Not God bless America! God damn America." Here is the key passage in Obama's Philadelphia speech:

I can no more disown him than I can disown the black community. I can no more disown him than I can my white grandmother—a woman who helped raise me, a woman who sacrificed again and again for me, a woman who loves me as much as she loves anything in this world, but a woman who once confessed her fear of black men who passed her by on the street, and who on more than one occasion has uttered racial or ethnic stereotypes that made me cringe. And they are part of America, this country I love. [Obama, 2008]

As Hertzberg (2008) observes: "Obama treats the American people as adults capable of complex thinking. . .But what made that speech special. . .was its analytic power. It was not defensive. It did not overcompensate. It is a combination of objectivity and empathy, it persuaded Americans of all colors that he understood them" (p. 40). This is no different from Lincoln's handling of slavery: "We can succeed only in concert. It is not can *any* of us *imagine* better, but can we *all* do better" (quoted in Miller, 2002, p. 224, italics in original).

These are lofty, profound, dramatic examples, but they are not different from what university leaders face in handling conflicts, whether it be race, left versus right, budget allocations, junior versus senior faculty, students' rights, and so on. We are talking about the qualities pertaining to leadership capacity for turnaround—a subject to which we turn in Chapter 5.

5

Leadership Capacity for Turnaround

L eadership is about *motivating* people, diverse people, to work together to get results never before obtained. It involves stimulating and tapping into energies hitherto dormant: "Leadership is not about making clever decisions and doing bigger deals, least of all for personal gain. It is about energizing other people to make good decisions and do other things. In other words, it is about helping release the positive energy that exists naturally within people. Effective leadership inspires more than empowers; it connects more than controls; it demonstrates more than it decides. It does all this by engaging—itself above all and consequently others" (Mintzberg, 2004, p. 143).

In this chapter, we capture the essence of turnaround leadership. We will see that it is about listening, linking, and leading (in that order) and about modeling, teaching, and learning. These new leadership qualities are identified in our Learning Leaders study (Scott et al., 2008). They are corroborated in the best research on leadership, and they have been exemplified over the years by leaders who create processes that reconcile seemingly impossible divisions, thereby creating new higher grounds of unity and prosperity.

The world of the academic leader, as we have seen, is wickedly challenging. There is a wide range of external change forces that continuously shift and bear down on our leaders. And then there are the many local change forces that can help or hinder necessary action. It is a world where change is inevitable, where the unexpected is to be expected, where leveraging talent to get action is critical, and where academic cultures, different traditions, and corporate goals can collide. What is important to understand is that, in this world, leadership cannot just come from the top. Everyone is a leader of change in their own area of expertise. It is a world where—if those who will implement a desired change do not see its relevance, desirability, and feasibility and if they are not clear on what they must do differently and are not helped to learn it—there is no change, only window dressing and plans with no implementation.

It is a world where, as a central or local leader, being able to regulate one's emotions—to remain calm when the unexpected happens or when confronted with passive aggression, to tolerate ambiguity, and to be undefensive and willing to listen and learn—is critical. It is world where being committed to the core purpose of beneficial student outcomes and being action-oriented and responsive while being able to make a hard decision counts. And it is a world where being able to empathize with others, work with diversity, listen, influence, get to the core of the issue, set priorities, diagnose what is going on, and design uniquely suited solutions with those who are to implement them also counts.

These are the factors, as we shall see, repeatedly identified in the Learning Leaders study (Scott et al., 2008) as crucial for effective turnaround leadership in universities and reinforced in workshops around the world. Yes, we must understand how to manage a budget, know how the university's HR processes work, and understand what makes for a sound learning program and how to engage students in productive learning. These competencies are necessary, but they are not sufficient for effective turnaround. Turnaround requires capabilities like those above, capabilities that bring together a distinct profile of emotional intelligence and cognitive ability.

Turnaround Leaders Listen, Link, and Lead

When change is in the air, when the unexpected inevitably happens, when conflict occurs, effective turnaround leaders in universities listen first, then link together what is learned and, only when this is done, do they lead. And they do this in partnership with those who will make the desired change work, always building on what is working elsewhere and in light of evidence of successful implementation and impact.

Listen

Turnaround leaders reach out to those who will make a desired change work with a well-argued, evidence-based case on why action in this area is necessary. Whenever possible, they listen with a "menu" of what has been done elsewhere (both within and beyond their university) to successfully address the focus area for improvement or strategic change that is on the table. This process of listening with a menu is important as it gives the process discipline and builds on a key factor for engaging staff—a reason to get involved and an indication that "fellow travelers" elsewhere have been able to make changes like this work.

Turnaround leaders actively invite people to identify within this framework of "steered engagement" what they believe is the most relevant, desirable, and feasible way to proceed. Their listening is authentic; that is, they really want to know what the people who will implement the change think will make it work best. They actively listen in order to identify, link, and distill the elements of a workable and productive plan of action, always testing this against what has worked elsewhere and in their own experience. They look for evidence that what staff (and students) are proposing is likely to be achievable and the most likely to best resolve the problem at hand. They understand that listening with discipline can help build motivation to own the problem and act, that it can also build a better solution than what they alone could design (many minds are better than one), and that it will build a plan of action that is not only relevant, understood, and owned but feasible.

Listening does not mean listening only to people who agree with you. It is just as important to listen to resisters. These people will always identify the road blocks that need to be addressed, and the very act of listening to them helps decrease their potential to become alienated and undermine implementation. If you listen carefully, resisters often have positive ideas.

Listening requires the ability to take one's ego out of the situation, to empathize, to tolerate ambiguity, and to take in ideas that don't align with yours. It also requires commitment and the cognitive skill to bring together a range of disparate ideas, to see the key issue and a way forward, and the ability to look not only at the technical dimensions of a turnaround situation but the human ones.

Link

Based on what they discover, on their diagnosis of the situation and their testing of the various options proposed for relevance, desirability, support, and feasibility, turnaround leaders make a decision on what is likely to work best. Then they check this with those who will implement the plan, by inviting them, against evidence, to make suggestions about what to add, drop, change, or highlight in the draft plan of action.

This work is not long-winded. The motto is, as we said in Chapter 4, ready, fire, aim; not ready, aim, aim, aim. Leaders check the emerging plan of action against their university's key turnaround agenda checkpoints like those identified in Chapter 3 and the key change management ones set out in Chapter 4, adjusting as they go.

Lead

A good leader, like a good teacher, actively involves those who will make the desired change work. The team knows that things won't work out exactly as planned, and the turnaround leader makes it clear that this is okay, that they are going to learn by doing. So, whenever possible, they try out the agreed plan under controlled conditions, monitor the results, learn what works, and change what doesn't. There is no defensiveness in this process. Everyone is willing to face aspects that don't pan out as anticipated, to figure out why, and to identify what might work better. They understand that students can be invaluable partners in this process.

So *lead* means acting in partnership through a rising spiral of learning by doing; it means trying the change under controlled conditions, evaluating its implementation and impact, retaining what works, and refining what doesn't until it is ready for scale-up. *Lead* means make sure that those who will act on the agreed plan are clear on what their role is, on how they will know if the change is working well, and how any shortcomings will be addressed. Just as students like clear expectations around learning, action, and assessment, so too do staff. Everyone likes to have some upfront, negotiated clarity on how the quality of what they have in mind will be judged and what tactics will be adopted to address any emerging shortcomings.

As the process of leading implementation unfolds, it is critical to distinguish between making judgments about the quality of inputs (such as the quality of the plan and making sure the right human and material resources are in place) and judgments about the quality of the outcomes (such as evidence that the desired change is working in practice and evidence that it is having a positive effect on the capabilities of those intended to benefit).

Turnaround Leaders Model, Teach, and Learn

We have found that turnaround leaders take on three critical roles. They intentionally model the change-capable culture they want their institution to develop; they teach their staff how best to implement a desired change; and they take on the role of learner, seeing what does and doesn't work in their area of responsibility, and they self-monitor their performance on the capabilities that distinguish effective leaders in universities, always seeking to improve in any areas found wanting.

Leader as Model

We have already argued that learning is a change process in which we develop the capabilities for productive and successful performance (Chapter 3), and that change is a learning process (Chapter 4). We have emphasized that the total experience can help or hinder learning for both staff, as they seek to implement a desired change, and students, as they learn and prepare for assessment. For students and staff the environment has, therefore, to be change-capable, focused, and aligned. That is, it has to help people learn from each other and from experience, and it has to be sufficiently efficient and unbureaucratic to give them room to learn.

What we found in our Learning Leaders study has been confirmed in workshops around the world. The ideal way to change a culture is for a critical mass of key leaders—centrally and locally—to intentionally model in their daily behaviors the attributes and capabilities they want the university to develop. People—our staff, friends, and, indeed, our own children—are influenced just as much by what we do as what we say. The listen, link, and lead strategy is a good example of what we are talking about.

Leader as Teacher

If change for staff and students is a complex learning and unlearning process, not an event; and if staff like to learn exactly how students like to learn (Chapter 3), then there is an important role for turnaround leaders in helping staff identify the gaps in their expertise necessary to deliver a desired change and then to fill them through a wide range of informal as well as formal learning strategies.

This work has links to the importance of leaders working together to build a change-capable culture, especially one where there are opportunities for peers to share successful practices in the areas of change being pursued. It also has direct links to shaping the development plans and performance reviews for staff and involves leaders in making sure that what is in these plans aligns with the key change priorities for their units. Finally, turnaround leaders work with centers of learning and teaching to make sure that their programs (both formal and informal) align with their staff's key change and learning needs.

Leader as Learner

We pursue this issue in more detail in Chapter 6 because it is critical to implementing the turnaround agenda. Leaders can't be left to their own devices to learn only by trial and error. We need to help them learn and build up their capabilities with focus, using a validated leadership framework for making sense of experience and to do so just-in-time and just-for-me. Just as students learn best through active learning, through experiencing the key dilemmas of real-world practice, through trying solutions and evaluating the results; just as students learn effectively through having just-in-time access to successful performers further down the same learning path, so too do our leaders.

Leaders who model a willingness to face and learn from their errors, who are interested in identifying where they can improve, and who strategically use networks with people in similar roles elsewhere to identify solutions to their personal improvement priorities simultaneously help build a dimension of a change-capable university culture we profiled in Chapter 4—a learning organization.

And, as we shall see in Chapter 6, universities need to more directly apply the learning designs and methods found to engage and retain their students in productive learning. In turn, learning programs for leaders must help these leaders learn by doing so that they can design learning experiences for other leaders and for their students.

Same Profile, Different Levels

What is surprising to us in all this research is how the profile of the change-capable graduate matches that of the effective teacher, the successful turnaround leader in a university, and leaders in other fields, including turnaround political leaders. What is equally surprising to us is how closely this profile characterizes change-capable cultures—both within higher education and beyond.

All leaders are able to self-regulate when things go wrong and be decisive and committed (a well-developed personal capability). All can empathize and influence (a well-developed interpersonal capability). All are able to diagnose, determine what is going on in a situation, get to the core of the issue, identify and trace out the consequences of potentially relevant courses of action, set priorities, determine what might work best with those who are to implement the chosen solution, and operate flexibly and responsively as implementation proceeds. These parallels concentrate the agenda for change-capable cultures and their leaders.

The Learning Leaders Study

The central role of leadership within a university is to frame the expectations of key actors to create the organizational settings in which knowledge can be grown, shared, and applied as a strategic resource. In this context, knowledge has a broad meaning, encompassing not just discipline knowledge but also knowledge specific to the organization in areas such as planning, workforce effectiveness, learning quality, productivity improvement, and change management, which must be developed and institutionalized within a strong community of practice model.

To do this, we review the findings of one of the largest studies of university learning and teaching leaders recently undertaken across the world, locate these findings within the broader leadership literature, and draw out the key implications for university leaders and their institutions (Scott et al., 2008). Once we understand what hundreds of academic leaders from across the world in the same role do to tackle challenges, how they leverage satisfactions and judge their performance, along with working to develop the capabilities which count most, university leadership becomes not just more manageable but exhilarating. With such knowledge we can, indeed, turn the tables on change. The research was undertaken through a partnership between the University of Western Sydney and the Australian Council for Educational Research (ACER) and was funded by the Australian Learning and Teaching Council (ALTC). It builds on a parallel study of effective leadership in education undertaken in 2003 (Scott, 2003) and applies a refined version of two conceptual frameworks tested in that study, one concerning leadership capability and the other concerning learning leadership.

The aims of the study were to:

- Profile university learning and teaching leaders in their roles as provost (deputy vice chancellor) and pro vice chancellor, dean and associate dean, head of school, department chair, head of program, learning and teaching director, and innovation team leader.

- Clarify what leadership actually means in the context of each role.

- Illuminate the daily realities, influences, challenges, and the most and least satisfying aspects of each role in order to give an insider's view of what life as an academic leader is currently like.

- Identify the key criteria which respondents in different roles use to judge the effectiveness of their performance.

- Identify the capabilities they see as being most important for effective performance in their role.

- Identify what forms of formal and informal support and learning are of most or least assistance in developing these capabilities.

- Determine where there are similarities and differences between the roles examined.

- Compare the findings with the existing literature on higher education leadership and those from parallel studies in other educational contexts.

The study involved an extensive literature review, feedback from agencies like the UK Leadership Foundation for Higher Education, analysis of a detailed online survey with more than 500 learning and teaching leaders, and one-on-one discussions with a subsample of these in 20 Australian universities covering all the leadership roles identified above. The findings were reviewed subsequently for their veracity and implications in a series of workshops with an additional 600 experienced academics and key senior players across Australia and internationally by higher education leaders in South Africa, Canada, the U.S., and New Zealand.

The Insider's Experience of Academic Leadership

One useful way to capture the insider's view of academic leadership in universities is to ask experienced leaders in different roles to identify an analogy for their work (Scott et al., 2008, p. 50). The most common of the 513 leadership analogies generated by the Learning Leaders study are presented in Table 5.1, sorted by role.

These analogies all indicate that the role of academic leader requires one to be able to negotiate not only constantly shifting external forces but also local ones; that leading is a complex, constantly changing, relatively uncertain, and highly human endeavor; that not everything can be preplanned or expected to turn out exactly in the way intended; that leadership is a team, not a solo

Table 5.1. Academic leaders' analogies

Most common across roles

Herding cats
Juggling

Senior leaders such as provost and dean

Being a gardener
Conducting an orchestra/directing a play
Keeping a flotilla heading in the same direction
Being the captain of a sailing ship
Coaching a successful sporting team
Climbing a mountain together
Plumbing a building—essential but no one sees it
Being a diplomat

Middle-level leaders such as head of department

Wearing multiple hats at the same time
Working with a dysfunctional family
Being the meat in the sandwich
Getting butterflies to fly in formation
Wading through a quagmire of bureaucracy
Having a Ferrari with no money for fuel
Trying to nail jelly to the ceiling while trying to put out spot fires with
    my feet
Trying to drive a nail into a wall of blancmange—little resistance but
    no result

Academic development directors and others
who must lead through influence

Being the older sibling in a large family
Being the minister of a church where only the converted come
Matchmaking
Bartending

(Continued)

Table 5.1. Academic leaders' analogies (Continued)

Junior leaders such as head of program

Being a small fish in a large cloudy pond
Being a salmon trying to swim upstream
Rowing without an oar
Sailing a leaky ship—faulty bilge pump
Pushing a pea uphill with my nose
Riding a bicycle on a tightrope
Being a one-armed paper hanger working in a gale

Others

Being in groundhog day
Living in a medieval castle
Being a Rubik's cube
Being in an Escher painting

effort; that culture (the way we do things around here) counts; that turnaround leadership can be frustrated by overly bureaucratic and unresponsive systems or by passive resistance; that, as the orchestra conductor analogy suggests, successful learning and teaching programs require both a sound plan (score) and people with the skills and ability to work productively together to deliver it in a harmonious and productive way (musicians).

The most popular analogies "herding cats" and "juggling" highlight the challenges of working with diversity and with the different tribes that make up the modern university. When the analogies are analyzed by role, it becomes clear that one's sense of efficacy shapes the type of analogy selected. It is also interesting to note a potential disconnect between the perceptions of the most senior leaders on how their organization and role operate and the perceptions of leaders lower down the hierarchy.

The implications of the analogies in Table 5.1 for organizational change in universities were discussed in detail at a series of national and international workshops. The main themes were:

- The local environment needs to be as efficient and focused as possible. Administrative processes need to be sharp, responsive, and demonstrably add value; there needs to be minimal duplication of effort; and meetings need to be well run and focused on action and delivering outcomes of clear benefit to students. In short, people need room to lead. As participants at one of the review workshops noted: "Wading through bureaucratic mud indicates the importance of sorting out the environment not just the people. Excessive bureaucracy and overly hierarchical approval processes indicate a lack of trust and an inability to sort out what really is of high risk and needs to be signed off at a number of levels and what can be made a local accountability. Responsiveness is key in the current environment and attending endless meetings or filling out templates without value-added is of no help."

- The way those local people who will actually implement a desired change and quality improvement in learning and teaching are involved needs considerable enhancement.

- There is a sense in the vast majority of analogies of people persevering, with moral purpose, in spite of all the frustrations.

- Analogies like "being in groundhog day" suggest the need for a more focused and clearly shared vision of where everyone is to head and that, as one respondent observed, "at present, the more things change the more they stay the same."

- The one-armed paper hanger and the jelly and blancmange analogies raised a critical issue for participants at the study's review workshops—how best to deal with a change averse culture (Chapter 2). These analogies, said participants, identify a unique challenge for leaders trying to engage university staff in the turnaround agenda—how to work with what a number called disengagement, white-anting, and passive resistance.

- Analogies like having to wear multiple hats indicate the need for clearer role focus.

- At one review meeting, it was noted that it is possible to see three ways in which the analogies vary: by role complexity and authority, by clarity of role, and by the level of resources available to the individual.

What these leadership analogies reveal is that we need people who are able to cope with the challenges of inevitable change and the unexpected, who can remain calm when it happens, who can read what needs to be done, and who can leverage their team's insights and skills to address each challenging situation in a harmonious way. This finding was reinforced when we asked our leaders to identify the indicators they use to judge that they are performing their role effectively.

The Satisfactions and Challenges of Being an Academic Leader

What became clear in the ALTC study and in the subsequent national and international discussions of its results is that, predictably, every leadership role has its fair share of both satisfaction and challenge. What emerged is that the most effective leaders know how to optimize the satisfactions and deal with the challenges in an informed, proactive, productive, and efficient manner.

The 513 leaders identified a recurring set of satisfactions. Understanding this is important for leadership motivation and retention. They varied to some extent, depending on the role concerned, as follows.

- Provosts and deputy vice chancellors reported finding satisfaction in setting strategy and direction, making team-based change happen, and interacting with clever, motivated staff.
- Deans found satisfaction in developing a productive group of leaders, helping staff achieve goals, formulating strategy, and implementing efficient systems.
- Heads of schools or departments found satisfaction in setting the direction for their unit, being able to make

things happen, assisting the development of their staff, and managing resources effectively.

- Heads of programs found satisfaction in assisting students, teaching, implementing new curriculum successfully, and building staff morale and skills.

- Directors of learning and teaching centers found satisfaction in working across the university to make desired learning and teaching improvements happen, in policy and strategy development, in identifying problems and addressing them, and in developing and assisting people to implement new approaches to learning and teaching.

The integrating theme in these satisfactions concerns working reciprocally and productively with staff to achieve real change. They also generally align with the key effectiveness indicators which respondents identified for each role. In terms of the most common challenges faced in different roles:

- Provosts and deputy vice chancellors reported that their major challenges centered around dealing with archaic processes, too much travel, attending meetings without an outcome, organizational indecisiveness, performance management of staff, and having to work with change-averse cultures.

- Deans reported having to educate bureaucrats, handle "administrivia," attend an excessive number of ritualized meetings, manage resource cuts, and deal with staff performance problems.

- Heads of schools or departments reported having to deal with "clunky" university processes, a continuous stream of ad hoc requests and meetings with little relationship to core business outcomes; a lack of recognition, reward, and praise for their achievements; and

having to manage escalated complaints, staff performance problems, and budget constraints.

- Heads of programs reported having to deal with dysfunctional systems and bureaucratic processes which
don't add value; difficult staff or staff inertia; and a
wide range of complaints from students.

- Directors of learning and teaching centers reported
having to lead through influence, work with unclear
role expectations, engage uninterested staff, undertake
continuous proposal writing, cope with continual
restructures of their area, attend unproductive meetings, and promote the equal status of learning and
teaching with research.

Delivering Turnaround Leadership—Identifying the Capabilities That Count

The ALTC study and subsequent reviews of its results around the
world have confirmed that an academic leader's capability is most
challenged when the unexpected happens, when a plan goes awry
and, in the distinctive context of a university, when faced by a
change-averse culture. When things are running smoothly, leadership capacity is untested. First a few words about the difference
between competence and capability, as the two concepts are often
conflated.

Competence

Competence is more associated with management, whereas capability is more associated with leadership. This generally aligns with
our review of the literature, where the concept of being competent
typically refers to someone who possesses the key skills and knowledge required to deliver the tasks that make up a specific job or are
necessary to run a particular operation effectively. The following
definitions are typical:

"Competencies are, in essence, definitions of expected performance that, taken as a whole, should provide users with the complete picture of the most valuable behaviors, values and tasks required for their organization's success." [Rankin, 2004]

"Competency means possessing the requisite capacities and knowledge base to undertake one's agreed upon functions." [Dauphin, 2005, p. 2]

Importantly, a sole focus on competency as the ability to perform set tasks to a specified standard fails to take into account the changing and uncertain nature of daily leadership practice or to emphasize the significance of an individual's capacity to know when and when not to draw upon specific areas of skill or knowledge. As Duignan (2004) concluded in his study, the requisite is having the "dynamic capacity to respond to changing circumstances and to try to improve those circumstances" (p. 7). And this requires something more than competence; it requires what, in this book, we define as "capability".

Capability

Capability is more associated with higher education leadership than management, with having the talent and capacity necessary to operate successfully to achieve continuous improvement and innovation. It entails attributes such as being able to work productively, calmly, persuasively, and deftly with diversity and uncertainty; a willingness to take responsibility and make hard decisions; a capacity to inspire others to action through sound decision making, integrity, and enthusiasm; an ability to diagnose and figure out what is really going on in a complex situation; and a capacity to see the big picture, to identify and set down what ultimately proves to have been a successful new direction, and to engage and support people in making it happen in a way that is both tactical and responsive. Capability involves, as one of our ALTC leaders pointed out, reading and responding to a rapidly changing external environment. In this perspective, capability sets the limits for both the development of competencies and their appropriate deployment, and it entails having the emotional and cognitive capacity to figure out when and when not to draw upon specific competencies, along with the capacity to learn from experience.

This view has links to Ramsden's (1998) observation that what combines aspects of leading and managing in higher education is leaders' capacity to manage not only their own learning and change but that of others: "(This) is closely associated with the idea of helping people through change and providing a vision for the future . . . It reflects an established notion in the mainstream literature on management and leadership—that effective leaders act as educators who help others learn . . . By these means credible leaders 'turn followers into leaders' (Kouzes & Posner, 1993, p. 156)" (Ramsden, 1998, p. 100).

Brungardt (1998) claims that collaborative leadership works best in postsecondary and higher education because it models what effective teachers do to help students learn. This notion of leader as model aligns with Martin, Trigwell, Prosser, and Ramsden's (2003, pp. 257–258) findings in their study of the links between university subject coordinators' leadership and teachers' approach to teaching: ". . . we have shown that the more collaborative approaches to the leadership of teaching at the individual subject level are associated with more conceptual, change-oriented and student-focused approaches to teaching. Given that other research has shown that these more conceptual change and student-focused approaches to teaching are associated with deeper approaches to learning (Trigwell, Prosser, & Waterhouse, 1999) this study would suggest that the way in which teachers experience the leadership of their departments is an important precursor to the quality of student learning processes and outcomes in their departments" (p. 2).

Thus, there are certain core capabilities and competencies common to turnaround leadership. We call this set of characteristics the leadership capability framework. Figure 5.1 identifies the conceptual framework for academic leadership capability, which guided the ALTC study and was tested, validated, and explained by it. It is directly based upon a framework already validated in studies of successful early career graduates in nine professions (Vescio, 2005) and in a detailed study of 322 effective school leaders (Scott, 2003) and is consistent with all of the literature reviewed above. It also has resonance with the graduate outcomes being sought by Sullivan and Rosin (2008) in the new agenda for higher education (Chapter 3).

Figure 5.1 identifies three overlapping aspects of leadership capability—personal, interpersonal, and cognitive. These domains are underpinned by two linked forms of skill and knowledge: generic competencies such as the ability to organize, run meetings, use IT, and understand how universities work; and role-specific competencies, in this case a high level of skill and understanding about learning and teaching in higher education.

The overlapping nature of the framework indicates that all five dimensions are necessary for effective performance as an academic leader and that the five domains identified feed into and off each other. For example, as noted earlier, we have clear evidence in the ALTC study and in those that have preceded it that a leader's capability is not tested when things are running smoothly but when something goes wrong, when something unexpected happens or, in

Figure 5.1. Academic leadership capability framework

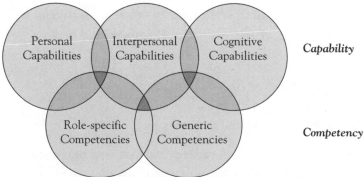

the unique context of higher education, when one is confronted by a change-averse or passive university culture.

Personal and Interpersonal Capabilities

At such times, it is important for leaders first to be able to manage their own emotional reactions to the uncertainty and discomfort, for example, not to overreact, to tolerate uncertainty, and to be able to remain calm. At the same time, as all key challenges of academic leadership have a human dimension, it is important to have a high level of interpersonal capability in order to better understand what is happening and sort out what might work best to resolve the situation.

The ALTC study produced and validated a set of personal and interpersonal capability items and scales that are important for effective turnaround leadership. They have considerable alignment with Goleman's (1998) concept of emotional intelligence.

Personal Capability

The components of personal capability identified as being most important for effective turnaround leadership are:

- *Self regulation*—the ability to defer judgment; an understanding of one's personal strengths and limitations; a willingness to admit to and learn from errors; being able to bounce back from adversity; maintaining a good work/life balance; and being able to remain calm under pressure or when things take an unexpected turn.

- *Decisiveness*—being willing to make a hard decision; being confident to take calculated risks; an ability to tolerate ambiguity and uncertainty; and being true to one's personal values and ethics.

- *Commitment*—having energy, passion, and enthusiasm for learning and teaching; wanting to achieve the best outcome possible; taking responsibility for program activities and outcomes; persevering when things are not working out as anticipated; and pitching in and undertaking menial tasks when needed.

Interpersonal Capability

The components of interpersonal capability that are most important for effective turnaround leadership are:

- *Influencing*—influencing people's behavior and decisions in effective ways; understanding how the different groups that make up one's university operate and affect different situations; working with very senior people within and beyond the university without being intimidated; motivating others to achieve positive outcomes; working constructively with people who are resisters or are over-enthusiastic; developing and using networks of colleagues to solve key workplace problems; and giving and receiving constructive feedback from work colleagues and others.

- *Empathizing*—empathizing and working productively with students and staff from a wide range of backgrounds; listening to different points of view before coming to a decision; developing and contributing positively to team-based programs; and being transparent and honest in dealings with others.

Cognitive Capability

The dimension of cognitive capability in Figure 5.1 refers to a leader's capacity to diagnose accurately what is happening when the unexpected occurs; to identify the human as well as technical, disciplinary, or administrative dimensions; to determine if the problem is worth addressing in detail; and then having the ability to match an appropriate course of action to this diagnosis. Donald Schön explored how this form of contingent intelligence operates in a wide range of occupations in his 1983 book *The Reflective Practitioner*. "When a practitioner makes sense of a situation he perceives to be unique, he sees it as something already in his repertoire . . . It is to see the unfamiliar situation as both similar to and different from the familiar one . . . The familiar situation functions as a precedent, or a metaphor, or—in Thomas Kuhn's phrase—an exemplar of the unfamiliar one . . . It is our capacity to see-as and do-as that allows us to have a feel for problems that don't fit existing rules" (Schön, 1983, pp. 138–40).

As we concluded in an earlier book *Change Matters* (Scott, 1999):

> Only when (change leaders) have a better handle on what the problem might really be. . .(do) they set about designing a way of changing the situation. . .That is, they seek to "custom tailor" or *match* a plan of action that seems to best suit the unique requirements, limits and possibilities of the situation. In this way their response is "contingent" upon their reading of the situation. . .Then they act—that is they put their plan into action and assess the effects. . .In this way they ultimately come to understand the problem only by trying to change it. If their selected solutions don't work, they conclude that their interpretation of the problem was inaccurate and the spiral starts again. In this way research, learning, action and workplace improvement are constantly inter-mingled in the "spiral staircase" of continuous change. [pp. 122–123]

Ramsden's studies (1998) of effective leadership also identified similar cognitive attributes to those noted above. They include being a strategic and contingent thinker, not a linear one; knowing what is achievable; having a clear but flexible vision and set of goals; and being able to plan ahead and not just be reactive (pp. 87–90). Based on these findings the ALTC study produced and validated a set of cognitive capability items and scales that are important for effective turnaround leadership. They are:

- *Diagnosis*—diagnosing the underlying causes of a problem and taking appropriate action to address it; recognizing how seemingly unconnected activities are linked; recognizing patterns in a complex situation; and identifying from a mass of information the core issue or opportunity in any situation.

- *Strategy*—seeing and then acting on an opportunity for a new direction; tracing out and assessing the likely consequences of alternative courses of action; using previous experience to figure out what is going on when a current situation takes an unexpected turn; thinking creatively and laterally; having a clear, justified, and achievable direction for one's area of responsibility; seeing the best way to respond to a perplexing situation; and setting and justifying priorities.

- *Flexibility and responsiveness*—adjusting a plan of action in response to problems that are identified during its implementation; making sense of and learning from experience; and knowing that there is never a fixed set of steps for solving workplace problems.

Clearly, a high level of interpersonal capability is necessary to undertake the process of reading and matching, and an ability to personally manage the uncertainty and ambiguity of an unresolved situation is needed if one is to be able to clearly and effectively think through what is causing it and figure out how best to respond. It is in this way that the three top circles in Figure 5.1 are interlaced, that is, one component cannot function without the other two being present.

Key Competencies

Also integrated into this process is a leader's level of generic and role-specific skill and knowledge (the bottom circles in Figure 5.1). These areas of competence provide not only a scaffold for diagnosis but also a source for shaping the right response and delivering it in partnership with all the other players concerned.

- *Learning and teaching*—understanding how to develop an effective higher education learning program; having a high level of up-to-date knowledge of what engages university students in productive learning; understanding how to design and conduct an evaluation of a higher education learning program; understanding how to implement successfully a new higher education program; being on top of current developments in learning and teaching; and knowing how to identify and disseminate good learning practice.

- *University operations*—understanding the role of risk management and litigation; understanding how universities operate; understanding industrial relations and processes as they apply to higher education; being able to help one's staff learn how to deliver necessary changes successfully; an ability to chair a meeting effectively; and having sound administrative and resource management skills.

- *Self-organization skills*—managing one's own professional learning and development; using IT effectively to communicate and perform key work functions; organizing one's work and manage time effectively; and making effective presentations to a range of different groups.

The framework in Figure 5.1 helps clarify how effective university leaders work with, learn from, and respond to changing circumstances. It allows that academic leadership is a highly contextualized phenomenon. It blends the competency and capability perspectives on leadership. It emphasizes that possessing a high level of skill and knowledge about how one's university operates or what makes for a productive approach to learning and teaching is necessary but is not sufficient for effective leadership in higher education. What is essential is the highly developed emotional intelligence and a contingent way of thinking that enables one to know when (and when not) to deploy (or add to) these competencies. It is in this way that Figure 5.1 shows how capability and competence, leadership and management are all necessary for effective turnaround leadership—the key priority in the operating context outlined in detail in Chapter 1.

Key Findings About Leadership Capability

In the ALTC study, the 513 leaders were asked to rank the 57 items that make up the above scales on their relative importance in the effective delivery of their role. The findings are discussed in detail in Scott et al. (2008, pp. 69–89). The overall findings have important implications for who we select as our university leaders and how we manage their performance evaluation and support. They highlight the capabilities such leaders will need to possess in order to deliver the turnaround agendas identified in Chapters 2, 3, and 4. The ALTC results show that:

No capability item attracted an importance rating of less than 3.9 out of 5 (1–low to 5–high).

Seven of the top ten items concerned emotional intelligence (personal or interpersonal), two concerned cognitive ability, and one concerned competence in time management.

Table 5.2 presents the 12 capability/competency items out of the 57 surveyed that ranked highest in importance by the leaders (their rank is indicated in brackets).

When a study of the ratings for specific aspects of capability was undertaken, a striking commonality from the most senior to the

Table 5.2. Top-Ranking Leadership Capabilities and Competencies

Emotional Intelligence (Personal)

Being true to one's personal values and ethics (2)

Remaining calm under pressure or when things take an unexpected turn (3)

Understanding my personal strengths and limitations (5)

Energy and passion for learning and teaching (7)

Admitting to and learning from my errors (10)

Emotional Intelligence (Interpersonal)

Being transparent and honest in dealings with others (1)

Empathizing and working productively with staff and other key players from a wide range of backgrounds (4)

Intellectual

Identifying from a mass of information the core issue or opportunity in any situation (8)

Making sense of and learning from experience (9)

Thinking creatively and laterally (11)

Diagnosing the underlying causes of a problem and taking appropriate action to address it (12)

Skills and Knowledge

Being able to organize my work and manage time effectively (6)

most junior leaders emerged. Irrespective of role, for example, aspects of emotional intelligence (personal and interpersonal) like those identified in Table 5.1 dominate, but always in combination with a contingent way of thinking and the appropriate use of a well-developed repertoire of relevant skills and knowledge. However, we also found that, as the scope, complexity, accountability, and seniority of the role grew, the more sophisticated, developed, and integrated all the dimensions of capability had to be.

We found that the focus of an academic leader's work influences the capabilities identified as being most important for effective leadership and that middle-level roles like head of school or department chair require a particularly powerful combination of capabilities because of the challenge of having to manage both up and down. We concluded that "the most demanding roles are indicated not only in the sorts of challenges identified, and the scope and level of accountability for the activities to be undertaken, but also in respondents' analogies. . . and their self identified effectiveness criteria" (Scott et al., 2008, p. 73).

Implications

The participants and reviewers of the ALTC project identified a number of potential ways in which the findings in this chapter might be implemented. Some concern what individual leaders might do and others concern what universities might do. The most common suggestions for individual leadership action are summarized below:

- Actively seek to implement the top 10 capabilities identified for each role—noting, in particular, the critical importance of emotional intelligence in achieving turnaround.
- When things go wrong, reflect using the capability framework and its specific scales and items to diagnose what might be causing the challenge. Then use this diagnosis to work with others in the same role to identify what they have done for development. Seek

feedback and try the approaches which others have found to work, evaluate the results, and, through this, learn by doing.

• Identify junior staff with leadership potential using the top 10 capabilities as a checklist and encourage them to take on leadership roles.

• Seek to consistently apply the listen, link, then lead strategy endorsed by so many effective leaders. Listening means reaching out to those who are to implement a desired change with a menu of potentially relevant solutions; seeking their input on the need, relevance, desirability, and feasibility of such a change; and asking them how, in their view, such a development might best be achieved. Link together these perspectives into an owned plan of action. And, lead by helping the staff to implement it. As one leader noted: "A leader's role is not unlike what teachers do in the classroom. Classroom management (teacher) is like organizational, team or staff management (leaders). Effective approaches to teaching and learning (the teacher) are like effective approaches to helping people learn to do agreed change and improve organizational outcomes (leader)."

• Consider the lessons identified by Julius, Baldridge, and Pfeffer (1999). They are all practical ways to implement the capabilities found to count most for turnaround leadership: operate with integrity, wisdom, and selflessness; build a team; concentrate your efforts; know when to engage conflict; learn the history of the issue; have a plan; use committees effectively; use the formal system; follow through to push the decision process; and be prepared to kill your own project when it has outlived its usefulness.

• Share the key findings from the ALTC study with colleagues and fellow leaders. Get the professional development unit to run a workshop on them and encourage the university or higher education system to replicate the study, thereby ensuring local relevance and that this is located within a broader, empirically tested framework.

• Make the link between graduate attributes and the key capabilities for leadership turnaround more explicit.

- Change your approach to those who are negative; listen to resisters, as they can provide a picture of the challenges that must be overcome to achieve successful implementation of a turnaround initiative and the act of listening to them is a positive act in its own right. Also actively compare notes with fellow leaders in the same role on how to most constructively handle difficult people. As one ALTC participant advised: Listen with greater tolerance to seemingly inconvenient suggestions.

- Confirm the validity of the position descriptions and the expectations given to one's reports.

- Alert staff to the fact that, when trying to implement a desired improvement, it is okay if things don't work out perfectly the first time through. Push, therefore, for a "why don't we" not a "why don't you" culture, emphasize that we "rise to great heights by a winding staircase," and make clear that we learn how to make change work by doing it.

- Actively model the capabilities that count, especially when things go wrong or when faced with passive resistance, knowing that this will help build a change-capable culture.

- Keep in mind that some leaders have to operate through influence, whereas others have more direct control because they have power over the distribution of resources; that is, some leaders have to use intrinsic motivators whereas others can use extrinsic ones.

- Realize how important it is to consistently communicate one's priorities and vision to staff. As one ALTC leader observed: "The cloudy pond"—is more the issue than the "bureaucratic mud". The mud is the sediment from the cloudy pond; the challenge is institutional indecision about teaching and learning.

In sum, keep in mind that, as a turnaround leader, one is a combination of teacher, model, and learner.

Additionally, a number of implications for universitywide action emerge. For example, the ALTC participants and reviewers emphasized that universities as a whole should:

• Critically review and validate position descriptions for all leadership roles against the findings in this chapter.

• Note the importance of leaders as models and builders of a change-capable culture of the type discussed in Chapter 4, and make targeted leaders accountable for this turnaround. Doing this is critical if we want to develop the sort of learning organization central to the successful implementation of the turnaround agenda identified in Chapter 3.

• Start the process of identifying future leaders now, using the findings of this chapter to focus the criteria that will be used.

• Ensure that professional learning for leaders focuses on the key areas for development in each role identified in this chapter; ensure that it models the flexible and responsive approaches to learning known to engage all adults and that this includes informal as well as formal elements.

• Focus, in particular, on key mediating roles like head of school, department chair, and head of program as it is these people who are the final arbiters of whether a turnaround change actually gets translated into daily practice by staff.

The emergence of President Barack Obama's leadership has helped to crystallize the turnaround leadership traits we have identified. As one conservative critic noted, Obama has "a first-class intellect and a first-class temperament" (in Hertzberg, 2008, p. 40), while Obama's rivals were consumed "with beating [the opposition] rather than unifying the country" (Lizza, 2008, p. 46). And, "this is a campaign where you need to respect other people's opinions" (Lizza, 2008, p. 50). Says another observer: "Obama has the capacity to inhabit different points of view" thereby having the "ability to negotiate among the sharply disparate perspectives of his fellow citizens" (Remnick, 2008, p. 79).

Confirming our point that turnaround leaders model and help others learn, Packer (2008) refers to Obama's philosophy of "deliberative democracy": "It denotes a conversation among adults who listen to one another, who attempt to persuade one another by means of argument and evidence, and who remain open to the possibility that they could be wrong" (p. 87). This is reminiscent of Pfeffer and Sutton's (2006) marvelous definition of wisdom: the ability to act with knowledge while doubting what you know (p. 17). Similarly Packer warns that, at its weakest, post-partisanship (listening to all sides) could "amount to an aversion to fighting" (p. 87). But turnaround leadership is a fight, pursuing relentlessly the moral purpose of fulfilling and improving people's lives. For turnaround leadership, the proof is in the pudding. Success will not occur through overpowering the opposition but rather by motivating and pressuring people to move to new heights.

A key aspect of this turnaround leadership is not trying to do everything yourself. It starts by building a team of learners who act as a guiding coalition through the consistent representation of the direction and the norms of conduct. As a newly appointed director of scheduling on Obama's team found when displaying irritation in a conference call, and received the prompt feedback after the call, "this is a campaign where you need to respect people's opinions and you can't be a bitch" (Lizza, 2008, p. 30).

This guiding coalition, led by the chief executive, in turn engages ever-widening circles of leadership. The point is that system change requires thousands of leaders. The more these myriad of leaders listen, link, and lead, and model, teach, and learn, the deeper and more sustainable the impact. Leadership is *not* a lonely proposition. Turnaround leadership is as social as it gets.

Thankfully the rest of us do not face Barack Obama's challenges. But, this is a difference in degree, not kind. Turnaround leadership in postsecondary institutions will require precisely the qualities we have been discussing in this chapter. Chapter 6 discusses how to look for and foster these qualities.

6

Leadership Selection and Learning

Our argument is that the development of academics into effective leaders requires explicit attention. We agree with Debowski and Blake (2004): "[There is] inadequate delineation of what leadership entails for those supporting teaching and learning in universities. . .the developmental needs of academic leaders should be regarded as a fundamental issue if universities are serious about improving their educational standards. . .universities need to invest in academic development to enable tailored support at specific strategic levels" (pp. 2, 8).

There is no good answer to the question of whether leaders are born or made. Some aspects of personal temperament accompany us as we enter this world, and certainly our early upbringing shapes our future behavior. At the same time, people can learn how to manage their emotions once they know what counts and are motivated to change. Either way, this makes leadership selection critical. In addition, developing leaders on the job, especially through mentoring and through creating learning opportunities, in context, is essential.

We get into some detail in this chapter about the selection and development of turnaround leadership. But remember the core focus we established in Chapter 5: listen, link, and lead, and model, teach, and learn carried out within the cognitive and emotional intelligence skills in our leadership capability framework.

Recall also the parallels and payoffs—the profile of the turn-around leader matches that of the change-capable organization, the effective teacher, and the effective graduate. All contribute to balanced leadership in society at a time when it is crucial to reconciling differences leading to greater individual and collective fulfillment. Higher education has a powerful role to play in the future beyond just the development of new knowledge, as important as that is.

If we agree on what needs to be done for turnaround leadership and if we have a clear profile of the capabilities leaders require to deliver it, then the next step is to make sure we are selecting the right people and assisting them in the most productive way to model and successfully lead implementation of the turnaround agenda.

Our research shows that the identification, selection, and development of our higher education leaders are generally not well managed. For example, the hundreds of university leaders involved in the ALTC study reported that selection often relies too much on a single interview, may not focus on the capabilities that count, and can concentrate on position descriptions that are not grounded in the capabilities required for change leadership. The following observations from the national and international discussions of the ALTC results are typical:

> If we were purchasing a piece of equipment worth a million dollars (the cost of some leaders over a three- to five-year contract), more effort would be given to deciding what to invest in than to reading a job application, asking around, and then having a 40-minute interview. Yet this can be what happens as we select new leaders. The cost of a bad appointment is not just the money—the cost flows through to the morale and productivity of many other staff.

> Environmental barriers to academic leadership include managerialism and the top-down selection of managers who may be chosen because they agree with superiors rather than for their ability to inspire staff.

> The good cook doesn't always make a great maitre d'.

> Hockey stars rarely make good coaches—they have spent their
> career thinking about how to make themselves best, not others.

The ALTC participants and reviewers also reported that their
experience with leadership development programs had generally
not been engaging, well-timed, sustained, or productive. This, they
said, is because these programs typically fail to focus on what counts
most in their role (the relevance test), that they tend to be one-off
and overly generic (the appropriate learning design test), and are
unsupported by a university operating environment conducive to
leading and learning (the context test).

The ALTC respondents were asked to identify how much of their
professional development had been devoted to enhancing the capabilities identified in Chapter 5. The results ranged from minimal to
moderate. This finding aligns with research undertaken elsewhere.
For example, Huntley-Moore and Panter (2003) report being able
to find little practical guidance on effective approaches to leadership
development or how it might best be implemented. Bass (1985,
1998) notes that academic leadership is often treated as a general
topic across disciplines and that the development of leadership skills
in the context of the institution or role in which it is practiced is
typically overlooked. Debowski and Blake (2004) found that leadership development for learning and teaching in universities is generally not well recognized, understood, or supported. Aziz et al.
(2005) and Montez (2003) found that leadership development as
well as selection is ad hoc. Gmelch's study of department chairs
found that most took up their role with no prior administrative experience or preservice leadership training (Gmelch & Miskin, 1993;
Gmelch, 2000). In a more recent review, Gmelch (2002) found that
only 3% of over 2,000 academic leaders surveyed in the U.S. between
1990 and 2000 had received any type of leadership preparation.

The good news is that most people who participated in the ALTC
study said they wanted to learn more about leadership. The better news is that if institutions of higher education take the matter

seriously, they will serve their students better—much better—while enhancing the scholarship, learning, engagement, and service mandates of their institutions.

As Chapter 5 shows and our work with experienced university leaders across the world confirms, effective change management and implementation are not only an increasingly central focus of university leaders' work, they are also among their top priorities for professional improvement. These leaders consistently say that they want to become better at leading culture change, learning and teaching change, and organizational change in ways that ultimately make a difference for our students. All of this augers well for turnaround leadership.

So what we are focusing on in this chapter is not just a matter of good leadership as an end in itself. We must understand learning leadership in its complexity and view it as a career-long learning process while always seeing it in the service of *leadership for what*. The turnaround agenda outlined in the previous chapters in this book furnishes the answer. This agenda is about: (1) focusing on knowledge that combines critical analysis and practical judgment in real-life situations; (2) making teaching and learning the centerpiece of postsecondary institutions and synergistically integrate them with research, community engagement, and service; (3) establishing quality reviews and evidence-based inquiry as the primary strategy for continuous improvement; and (4) building leadership whose strength is carrying out the agenda contained in the previous three items. In this latter respect, what works for institutions works for individuals. That is, change-capable institutions are made up of change-capable individuals, especially change-capable leaders.

The majority of universities do not now take this agenda seriously. It is not that they have deliberately rejected it. They just don't know it. Failure to realize this places postsecondary institutions at the mercy of their environments. Survival is always a matter of engaging your environment as lead learners. The shift in university cultures to take leadership identification, selection, and learning seriously will not be an easy one. It involves developing our leaders as models, teachers, and learners; starting succession planning early; using relevant, online leadership learning systems for staff to self-assess and develop against; making professional development role-specific and valid; and shaping an environment that gives people not only room to lead but also room to learn. In a word, leadership selection and learning must become the new priorities for universities and colleges.

Refocus Leadership Selection and Succession Planning

The following observations from national and international discussions of the ALTC project are typical:

> An academic culture is a difficult environment to work with in initiating and implementing change. As a leader this makes it particularly challenging—a good leader will thrive on such a challenge. Let's select the right people into specific positions—not just because they have a PhD (or a great research record).

> We have recognized the importance of generic capabilities for our students but this is not mirrored for staff (i.e., we don't select and reward staff for their emotional intelligence).

If we are to address the leadership succession crisis that is now bearing down upon our universities and put in place people who can address the turnaround agenda, then it is critical to focus more carefully on the effectiveness indicators and the key leadership capabilities identified as being critical in Chapter 5 as we identify potential leaders and determine which of them should be appointed to particular leadership roles. For this to happen, it is necessary to critically review the position descriptions and performance criteria currently used for leadership roles all the way from provost to head of program for their validity, relevance, and complementarity against, for example, the findings in Chapter 5.

The traditional approach to leadership selection requires review to confirm that the position description and capabilities given focus are indeed necessary to the role being considered in terms of who is on the committee; to validate the questions and tests that will be used; and to establish the extent to which the formal interview is part of a more triangulated set of mechanisms that will be used to confirm that the person finally selected is, indeed, the right one. A particular challenge is to figure out how best to measure the key aspects of emotional intelligence and cognitive capability identified as being critical for turnaround leadership.

As Julius, Baldridge, and Pfeffer (1999) observe in their tongue-in-cheek memorandum from Machiavelli to U.S. senior administrators and faculty leaders who are seeking change:

> Be wary of a search committee's propensity to find the right people. Search committees often recommend those who are acceptable to the group (or those who may offend the fewest)! Assembling a team requires you to resist strong pressures to appoint "traditional" individuals.
>
> Traditionalists are not often comfortable with nor do they usually understand how to manage "change" or "conflict." Go outside of the traditional realm. The appointment of excellent and supportive academic administrators will be a task to which you should devote attention. Do not assume a search committee will simply do what you ask. Check the details of "who" serves on the committee, the charge of the committee, read the position description before the position is advertised. [pp. 118–119]

Finally, it is also important to confirm that the same areas of focus, effectiveness, and capability that are used to select staff are being used for their performance assessment and development as they deliver their leadership role. In this regard, there are important implications in the ALTC study concerning the need to validate the items in the wide range of 360-degree feedback systems currently being used in higher education around the world.

Learning Leadership—Focusing on What Counts

When the leaders in the ALTC study were asked to identify the criteria they most use to judge that they are performing their role effectively, they were also asked to identify which of these was a professional development priority. Table 6.1 gives the results.

In column one, we have given the ranking (1 highest) on how important our respondents believed performance in each of these areas was to judging their effectiveness. In column two of this table we have given the ranking (1 = highest) for the top five priorities for professional development identified by the ALTC respondents.

Table 6.1. Professional development priorities × leadership effectiveness criterion

Effectiveness criterion	Importance in judging effectiveness (1 = high)	Priority for further professional development (1 = high)
Achieving high-quality graduate outcomes	1	5
Successful implementation of new initiatives	2	4
Producing significant improvements in learning and teaching quality	3	3
Establishing a collegial working environment	4	2
Achieving a high profile for my area of responsibility	10	1

The areas attracting high rankings in both columns are establishing a collegial working environment, producing significant improvements in learning and teaching quality, successful implementation of new initiatives, and achieving high-quality graduate outcomes. Although achieving a high profile for one's area of responsibility attracts a high rating for development, it attracts a much lower ranking on importance as a criterion for judging effectiveness.

Not only do our leaders across all roles identify the areas above as being a relevant focus for learning leadership, people in particular leadership roles select additional ones. For example, provosts also give priority to developing their ability to bring innovative policies and practices into action; deans, to achieving positive outcomes from external audits; and associate deans, directors, and heads of programs to achieving significant improvements in learning and teaching quality.

There is some alignment between these findings and research elsewhere on the learning needs of leaders in higher education. For example, the research of Aziz et al. (2005) with department chairs in U.S. universities found that their professional learning priorities were (in rank order): (1) the ability to deal with and provide feedback to unsatisfactory staff; (2) knowledge of policies, procedures, and funding sources; (3) skills to reduce, resolve, or prevent conflict among faculty members; and (4) developing the ability to use different leadership styles to fit varying situations.

Ensuring That Leadership Learning Is Productive and Engaging

Leadership courses can be helpful, but it is learning on the job—purposeful learning in context—that really counts. Ramsden (1998) reinforces this point: "We delude ourselves, though, if we think we can specify precise competencies and then train academic leaders in the practice of these competencies, perhaps in a short orientation or in-service course. Leadership is a balancing act. We might wish it were systematic and predictable; in reality it is disordered and episodic, and each leader's history is scattered with omissions, confusion and failures. . .This task cannot be taught. It can only be learned by doing the job, seeking feedback and instruction from colleagues, actively interpreting that information, and doing the job again" p. 254).

Extensive evaluation research of staff development in education over the past twenty-five years confirms that the same factors engage students and staff in productive learning. These factors were identified in Chapter 3 and are summarized below.

- The total experience produces effective learning and change, not just what happens in formal workshops, classes, and meetings.

- Learning is a profoundly social experience, and one's peer group is a powerful factor in helping or hindering engagement.

- Learning (what students and staff do and how they change) is not teaching (what lecturers and leaders do to assist this learning).

- Active learning methods can engage people and ensure that their learning is productive.

- Assessment and feedback (self-managed and from others) is the engine house of learning, especially if it focuses on developing the capabilities known to count most for effective performance in a particular role by identifying gaps in these capabilities and directly suggesting proven ways to address them.

- Self-managed learning linked to timely, solution-focused feedback is a key element in this process, especially when it addresses an experienced problem or dilemma of real-world practice.

When taken together, these factors can be consolidated into a set of quality assurance checkpoints. We have used the "Rated Class A" quality assurance framework for ensuring that leadership learning in higher education is both engaging and productive.

Rated Class A Framework and Checkpoints

R-Relevance

Confirm that the content and focus of the leadership program is immediately relevant to the backgrounds, abilities, needs, and experiences of the leaders concerned.

A-Active learning

Use an appropriate mix of the active learning methods identified as a best aspect in many studies of learning in postsecondary and higher education (Table 3.1). More than 60 such learning methods and tactics have been identified. They include almost 40 face-to-face and practice-oriented methods (group work, debates, forums, seminars, field trips, work placements, site visits, and use of guest speakers, etc.); a wide variety of simulation techniques (case studies, in-tray exercises, role play, etc.); self-managed learning resources (assessment-focused self-teaching booklets and distance education materials); IT-enabled learning strategies (teleconference, video, CD, podcasts, Skype, YouTube, various Web-learning products, SMS, online library search and downloads, etc.); and a range of peer-supported learning systems.

T-Theory-practice links

Consistently use practical, real-world problems, experiences, and cases to test and inform theory, and use practice, whenever possible, as a site or source for learning. The use of problem-based assessment methods, rather than simply testing factual recall, is especially important.

E-Expectations management

Ensure clear management of expectations from the outset on what levels of service, support, and contact participants are entitled to, along with what they are expected to do, with particular emphasis on how any performance assessment associated with the program will be managed and participants' obligations in relation to it.

D-Direction and coherence

Ensure clarity about where a leadership learning program is heading and how its various elements make up a coherent whole. Staged feedback and vertical integration of learning and assessment are also important ingredients in ensuring clear direction.

C-Capabilities that count

To achieve relevance, focus on the capabilities known to count most for effective performance in the first five years of professional practice in the leadership role concerned. A high level of technical and practical skill is necessary, but it is not sufficient for effective leadership performance.

L-Learning pathways that are flexible

Participants like both clear direction and a core set of key learning activities to develop the necessary capabilities. However, they also like the ability to take electives that suit their particular interests.

A-Assessment

Assessment of what has been learned is key to an engaging and effective leadership learning program. Assessment needs to be valid (to focus on the capabilities that count) but also to test capabilities using integrated and problem-based assessment, rather than testing factual recall. Learners see prompt and constructive feedback on what might have been done to achieve a higher level of performance against effectiveness indicators like those identified in Chapter 5 as constituting a unique opportunity for individualized learning.

S-Staff

The program staff, both academic and general, need to be experienced leaders and teachers—flexible, accessible, responsive, and enthusiastic. Leadership program staff need to take on the role of being a learning designer, the so-called "guide on the side" rather than the "sage on the stage." They need to see their role, therefore, as designing active and responsive learning systems focused on enabling participants to complete carefully integrated and problem-focused assessment tasks. Administrative and support staff play a key role in ensuring learning programs are consistently and effectively supported during their delivery.

S-Support

This includes ensuring that a responsive and efficient program administration system is in place; that there is an easily accessed online library and a relevant range of learner support opportunities; and that peer support is actively developed and assisted.

A-Access

Convenient times and locations for learning are important factors for many leaders. They typically have to balance complex work and family obligations with study.

A key insight that has emerged from our research on what engages our leaders in productive learning is that, if we can help them experience what we know engages higher education students in productive learning and retains them, then we will concurrently achieve three key objectives for turnaround:

- The learning of the leaders will be productive.

- They will experience firsthand what they need to advocate their staff do to engage their students in productive learning.

- They will experience how to build a more change-capable culture in the context of their learning.

Leadership Learning Scales

In the ALTC study, the above research was brought together into a set of academic leadership development scales. These are summarized in Table 6.2.

The 513 ALTC respondents were asked to rank these items in terms of their effectiveness in helping them develop their capabilities as an academic leader. At the scale level, the results show that most leaders express a preference for practice-based learning, followed by self-managed learning, and finally formal development activities. The relatively low ratings for the more formal development activities may be due to their poor conception, not their intrinsic worth. This issue requires further exploration.

In terms of specific learning methods, the highest ranking approaches were (in rank order): (1) learning on the job; (2) ad hoc conversations about work with people in similar roles; (3) participating in peer networks within a university; (4) being involved in

Table 6.2. Approaches to academic leadership development and learning

Scale	Item
Self-managed learning	Ad hoc conversations about work with people in similar roles
	Participating in peer networks within the university
	Participating in peer networks beyond the university
	Undertaking self-guided reading on leadership
	Accessing leadership information on the Internet
	Involvement in professional leadership groups or associations

(Continued)

Table 6.2. Approaches to academic leadership development and learning (Continued)

Scale	Item
Practice-based learning	Involvement in informal mentoring or coaching
	Involvement in formal mentoring or coaching programs
	Undertaking work placements or exchanges
	Participating in leadership development programs that are tailored to one's needs
	Study of real-life workplace problems
	Undertaking site visits to other institutions or agencies
	Learning on-the-job
Formal leadership development	Participating in 360-degree feedback reviews based on known leadership capabilities
	Participating in higher education leadership seminars
	Completing formal leadership programs provided by your university
	Completing formal leadership programs given by external providers
	Attending learning and teaching conferences
	Completing a tertiary qualification relevant to leadership
	Participating in annual performance reviews

informal mentoring and coaching; (5) study of real-life workplace problems; (6) participating in peer networks beyond the university; and (7) undertaking self-guided learning. This research has enabled us to identify what an overall leadership learning system in higher education might focus on. This is represented in Figure 6.1.

This figure suggests that professional learning for academic leaders should follow an action learning cycle in which a combination of proven formal, practice-based, and self-managed learning methods are used. This learning cycle involves an ongoing process in which the gaps in one's capability are identified using the leadership scales and dimensions confirmed in Chapter 5 (diagnose). These gaps are then addressed using a mixture of self-managed learning, practice-based learning, and appropriately timed and linked formal leadership development activities (develop). As this is undertaken, the results are monitored using effectiveness indicators like those identified in Table 6.1 (implement and monitor), and judgments about the quality of what has emerged are made (evaluate). Areas of good practice are retained, and those requiring further attention and new gaps for development are readdressed. In this way, the cycle continues. The key is to see the process as not only cyclical but as heading to somewhere significant by using the validated capability and focus scales identified in Chapter 5. As noted earlier, this notion was captured well by Francis Bacon when he observed, "We rise to great heights by a winding staircase."

A key recommendation of the ALTC respondents and reviewers was for the development of an IT-enabled learning resource which permits current or new leaders in higher education to learn in their own time and to access what experienced leaders in their role have discovered about the capabilities that count most for effective practice, along with the key challenges for their particular role and how best to address them.

Such an online leadership learning system (OLLS) is currently being developed and implemented in Australia. It has a number of

Figure 6.1 Academic leadership learning system

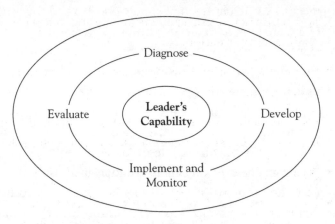

Formal Leadership Development	Practice-based Learning	Self-managed and informal learning
• 360-degree programs • Higher education leadership seminars • Leadership programs run by university • Leadership programs run by external groups • L&T conferences • Completion of a tertiary qualification in leadership	• Mentoring • 'Shadowing' • Work placements • Exchanges • Custom-tailored learning programs • Study of real-life problems and cases • Visits • Learning 'on the job' • Secondments • Use of 'teaching fellows'	• Peer group • Network in university • Network beyond university • Internet • Professional association

key characteristics and uses. In terms of its key characteristics, it applies key findings on how IT-enabled learning can best be used as part of the broader learning system outlined in Figure 6.1. For example, it:

• Provides access to the learning of experienced people in the same role, rather than simply giving unsituated information.

- Provides information just-in-time and just-for-me.

- Focuses on active engagement in learning, not passive reading of information.

- Provides a one-stop shop for information relevant to effective practice.

- Uses problem- and case-based learning generated from the real-world experience of leaders in particular roles.

- Is easy to operate and simple to navigate.

- Includes the original questionnaire used in the ALTC project. Users can complete this and immediately get back their results compared with those of hundreds of other leaders in the same role who have already filled out the survey.

- Uses an active database, not a passive one. Input from new users is moderated and used to build up a situated learning exchange for leaders in each university role.

In terms of how OLLS can be used, any one or mix of the following is possible:

- A new or existing leader completes the questionnaire, privately reflects on the results for their role, and considers the relevant case studies and suggested ways of handling them.

- A person interested in applying for a particular leadership role uses the system to identify what the role entails and self-assesses against the survey results for that role.

- One's results on the leadership questionnaire can be used with a mentor to discuss targeted development plans, either in a current role or as an aspirant to a new one.

- The OLLS tool can be used as part of a more formal leadership development program by having all participants complete the questionnaire for their role, pool their results, compare them with experienced leaders in that role, and then discuss the outcomes at a workshop.

In a word, leadership programs need to become personalized in the context of the basic qualities of our leadership capability framework. We have argued that university leaders in every role, from the president, vice chancellor, and provost to department chair and course leader, is a leader of change in his or her own area of expertise. We have suggested that this work needs to be more intentional, coordinated, and led from the top in a partnership with the line staff and leaders. Partnership with local leaders in faculties and divisions—listening, then linking and leading—is critical because it is these local people who are, after all, the final arbiters of whether a desired change actually gets put into practice. Why? Because local leaders choose or do not choose to engage their staff in implementing any proposed change; it is local leaders who will help their staff learn the gaps in their expertise necessary to deliver such changes.

It is equally important for the most senior leaders in our universities to lead by example; to actively determine the extent to which their university has the attributes of a change-capable learning organization; and to review their university's leadership position descriptions to make sure they are valid, complementary, and focused on what counts for the sustainable future of their institution.

Our study has shown the complexity of change, but it has also unpacked its main components. We now have a clearer agenda for developing leadership learning and, we would venture to say, a growing interest on the part of potential leaders to partake in this agenda. This opportunity is especially compelling because developing learning leaders and the core purposes of universities in today's global society overlap in significant ways. One does not leave learning to lead. Learning and leading are symbiotic.

Now all we have to do is to get down to the business of changing university cultures by integrating learning and leading—a tough but attractive proposition.

7

Lead, Lead, Lead

When we told one of our colleagues that we were writing a book on turnaround leadership in universities, he responded in a nano second, "It will be easier for Obama to turn around the U.S." We will leave that for the future, but we do know two things. It *will* be extremely difficult to bring about the required changes, but there is a strong interest in moving down the path we have outlined, with some institutions already well into the journey. In this chapter we will review the content of the reform we are advocating, revisit the change process and the kind of leadership that will get us there, and end with why society and higher education need each other for the next phase of development.

The Content of the Reform

We made the case in Chapter 3 that universities need to concentrate their efforts and that they need an integrator in order to focus on what only they can do best. We suggested that this integrator be a new and radically different focus on teaching and learning. As such, the role of higher education is not to impart knowledge, and not even to develop critical thinking as an end in itself, but to help students make judgments based on a combination of analytic insight and responsible reasoning applied to typical and intractable problems that they and others inevitably face in real life.

We suggested that this is best achieved by focusing on (1) practical reasoning, a more integrated conception of the role of knowledge that combines analysis and application; (2) putting teaching and learning at the center of the traditional triumvirate of research, teaching, and engagement; (3) the university turning inquiry on itself to establish quality processes, data, and implementation; and (4) building the corresponding leadership capacity within universities based on theory and knowledge. This new role is not just a matter of improving teaching. It goes to the guts of the conception and role of knowledge in the postmodern world. It takes knowledge out of the laboratory (although there will and should be basic research) and into the field of addressing complex problems faced by complex societies. The focus on practical, knowledge-based reasoning produces better graduates *and* better theories. We noted that many universities were already well advanced in implementing this new model in particular courses, but far fewer were doing so at an institutional level.

There is a great synergy and parallelism in this work across three components: students as learners, teachers as learners, and graduates entering the world of work and citizenry. All three become change-agents fit for purpose. They solve problems based on past knowledge, cross-disciplinary perspectives, reciprocal partnerships, and novel applications generated by the issues they face in their daily lives. The heart of this work is knowledge, including its cognitive and emotional depths. Universities are especially suited to make what Sullivan and Rosin (2008) called "shaping the life of the mind for practice." Teaching with this goal at the center becomes the new laboratory of the university. This represents an exciting but very deep change for many postsecondary institutions.

Change-Savvy Leadership

We will need leaders at all levels of the university who can engage in combining analytical and emotional knowledge in the service of morally robust reform.

The tendency of universities to be rational, and in some cases hyperrational, has not served them well. Among the myths of change are:

- The brute logic myth: *All I have to do is give them the case for change and they'll engage.*

- The consensual myth: *We won't change if we don't all vote in favor of what is being proposed.*

- The academic independence myth: *I'm not interested in this new managerial stuff; my job is to do my research, not attend meetings.*

- The knight on the white horse myth: *All will be well now that we've appointed a new president.*

- The linear myth: *Change unfolds in a neat, linear way from plan to implementation.*

- The restructure myth: *When in doubt, restructure. This is all we need to make the university a success.*

- The task force myth: *Let's get the best minds in the place to figure this out.*

- The strategic plan myth: *The hard work's done, the plan is launched. Now all you've got to do is implement it.*

As one of our colleagues wryly concluded in his research, "the size and prettiness of the plan is inversely related to the quality of action" (Reeves, 2006, p. 64).

Fortunately, there is a great deal of practical, deep knowledge available on understanding and leading change. We presented the findings in Chapter 5 from our study of leaders in higher education. The essence of our conclusion was that effective leaders combine certain capabilities (personal, interpersonal, and cognitive) and competencies (role-specific and generic skills) to manage change effectively

(Figure 5.1). Faced with demanding situations, they remain cool, empathize, understand differences, and work to find solutions through joint action. In particular, they listen, link, and lead, and model, teach, and learn themselves. They hone these capabilities as continuous learners, and, above all, they foster these leading learning capacities in others, always generating leaders for the future.

But here let's take these ideas a step further and consider turnaround leadership. Turnaround leaders are those who find themselves faced by expectations (at least by those who hired them) to make fundamental change. Whether you are a newly appointed deputy vice chancellor, president, provost, dean, or department head, the dilemma that our change leader faces is the "too-fast, too-slow" conundrum. If he or she moves too fast, the culture rebels, and, more times than not, the leader leaves. Moving too slowly usually results in the new leader getting absorbed by the culture and nothing much happens (the more things change the more they remain the same). Change-savvy leaders work at managing this balance in dynamic equilibrium. We especially like Herold and Fedor's (2008) advice in their *Changing the Way We Lead Change*. In a kind of "you only get to make a first impression once," they recommend:

- Careful entry into the new setting
- Listening to and learning from those that have been there longer
- Engaging in fact-finding and joint problem solving
- Carefully (rather than rashly) diagnosing the situation
- Forthrightly addressing people's concerns
- Being enthusiastic, genuine, and sincere about the change circumstances
- Obtaining buy-in for what needs fixing
- Developing a credible, owned plan for making that fix (pp. 47–48)

Of course, this is easier said than done, and there are a myriad of details, but our own framework of leadership capabilities is essentially compatible with this advice. It is also fundamentally congruent with our "six secrets of change" based on evidence of effective organizations in a variety of sectors (Fullan, 2008a). Change-savvy leaders combine and integrate the nuances of the six secrets: (1) love your employees as well as your customers; (2) use purposeful peer interaction to change cultures; (3) emphasize capacity building over judgmentalism; (4) know that learning is the work: (5) embrace transparency of both practice and results; and (6) invest in system learning through collaboration. Leading change via the six secrets is about managing paradoxes and reconciling dilemmas. It is about constantly figuring out how best to balance stability and change; top-down and bottom-up approaches; listening and leading; and looking inside and outside for change ideas and solutions.

There is a pattern here. Effective change leaders have high moral purpose, but they don't try to impose it on others. They proactively engage in learning processes that end up reconciling divisions and motivating joint action. Because this is dicey, especially at the beginning, these leaders work through the difficult early period without panicking. Consider the early stages of a complex change process. A universal finding in all cases of change, including eventual successes, is the implementation dip. At the beginning of a change process, the costs to individual implementers is high, immediate, and palpable (because they are not skilled at or understanding of the new way), and the rewards are distant and theoretical. Change-effective leaders acknowledge this reality and take actions (such as capacity building) to limit (but by definition not eliminate) the length of the implementation dip. Because this is an uncomfortable period, change effective leaders know one thing for sure: as a leader during this phase, do not expect many compliments. They stay the course while solving problems early.

There is one other overriding quality evidenced by effective change leaders. Here is the dilemma. On the one hand, the future is intrinsically unpredictable (complexity theory), and, on the other hand, people want a degree of certainty. Leaders without the change capabilities we have identified make one of two mistakes. Some suffer from, or rather their followers suffer from, the consequences of the leaders' certainty. Being prematurely decisive in the face of complexity can be fatal. By contrast, other leaders, humble as they are, become overwhelmed by the chaos and retreat into immobilized inaction. Effective change leaders know that sometimes they have to act with more confidence than the situation warrants. They reflect what we cited earlier as Pfeffer and Sutton's (2006) definition of wisdom: "using your knowledge while doubting what you know." Because they practice and hone their change leadership capabilities, they in fact do know a great deal—but not everything, so they keep on leading and learning with both confidence and humility.

Society and Higher Education Need Each Other

We don't give the usual answer here. Of course, society needs an increasingly highly skilled work force and citizenry. But more than that, global society needs people who engage with others, shaping the future through solving complex problems together with all the analytic and emotional intelligence that can be mustered. We need, in other words, lead learners who serve as agents of change by preserving the best of the past as they help forge a new and more complex future.

You don't have to go to university to do this, but our argument is that universities are especially well placed to contribute to society in this way and that this role represents their best future. The economist Paul Romer (2004) observed that "a crisis is a terrible thing to waste." We made the case in Chapter 1 that universities are already facing a combination of severe crises. These and other crises have become universal—all countries, all walks of life, all institutions. This presents a golden opportunity for higher education to redefine itself not to resolve its own future but as part and parcel of healthy, prosperous societies.

The new mission is clear, exciting, and right in the wheelhouse of the best traditions of universities—generating in all of its graduates leaders who have thought through what they stand for, who can work constructively with diversity, and who can learn. Higher education institutions should be leading by going much beyond their knowledge agenda into the learning agenda in the deepest meaning of the latter. In so doing, they will achieve a double payoff. Not only will they optimize the chances that the desired changes will succeed and be sustained, they will also be modeling to their learners and colleagues the values central to a civil society.

This takes us to the bottom line and the core message of this book. It is time that leaders in higher education put their minds and hearts—their institutions—into this grander and absolutely crucial agenda. No other institution is as well placed to make such a multifaceted contribution. Think of society, think of the world. Listen, link, and lead; model, teach, and learn! This is the essence of turnaround leadership.

References

Abrahamson, E. (2004). *Change without pain*. Boston: Harvard Business School Press.

Arizona State University (ASU). (2008). *A new American university*. Tempe: Arizona State University. [http://mynew.asu.edu/downloads/New_American_University_July2005.pdf]

Aziz, S., Mullins, M., Balzer, W., Grauer, E., Burnfield, J., Lodato, M., & Cohen-Powless, M. (2005). Understanding the training needs of department chairs. *Studies in Higher Education, 30*(5), 571–593.

Barr, R., & Tagg, J. (1995, Nov.-Dec.). From teaching to learning. *Change*, 13–25.

Bashir, S. (2007). *Trends in international trade in higher education: Implications and options for developing countries*. Washington, DC: The World Bank. [http://siteresources.worldbank.org/EDUCATION/Resources/278200-1099079877269/547664-1099079956815/WPS6_Intl_trade_higherEdu.pdf]

Bass, B. M. (1985). *Leadership and performance beyond expectations*. (3rd ed.) New York: Free Press.

Bass, B. M. (1998). *Transformational leadership: Industrial, military and educational impact*. Mahwah, NJ: Erlbaum.

Bergquist, W., & Pawlak, K. (2008). *Engaging the six cultures of the academy*. San Francisco: Jossey-Bass.

Blackmore, J., & Sachs, J. (2000). Paradoxes of leadership and management in higher education in times of change: Some Australian reflections. *International Journal of Leadership in Education, 3*(1), 1–16.

Bligh, D. (2000). *What's the use of lectures?* San Francisco: Jossey-Bass.

Bok, D. (2006). *Our underachieving colleges: A candid look at how much students learn and why they should be learning more*. Princeton, NJ: Princeton University Press.

Bollaert, L., et al. (eds.). (2007). Embedding quality culture in higher education. Brussels: First European Forum for Quality Assurance, EUA. [http://www.eua.be/fileadmin/user_upload/files/Publications/EUA_QA_Forum_publication.pdf]

Boyer, E. (1990). *Scholarship reconsidered: Priorities of the professoriate*. Princeton, NJ: Carnegie Foundation for the Advancement of Teaching.

Brown, L. R. (2008). *Plan B 3.0: Mobilizing to save civilization*. New York: Norton.

Brungardt, C. (1998). *The new face of leadership: Implications for higher education*. Leadership Studies, Fort Hays State University.

Campus Review. (2007). Views and characteristics of senior officers in Australian universities. Report prepared by APN Educational Media. Sydney, Australia: Author.

Cech, S. (2008). Gates sets sights on higher college completion rates. *Education Week, 28*(13), 10.

Chronicle of Higher Education. (2008). [www.chronicle.com/weekly/oct10]

Cox, E. (1995). *A truly civil society*. Sydney, Australia: Boyer Lectures, ABC.

Daniel, J. (2007, February). The expansion of higher education in the developing world: What can distance learning contribute? Washington, DC: CHEA International Commission Conference.

Dauphin, B. (2005). Letter on competency for psychologists. *The Michigan Society for Psychoanalytic Psychology, 15*(2).

Debowski, D., & Blake, V. (2004). The developmental needs of higher education academic leaders in encouraging effective teaching and learning. Seeking Educational Excellence, Teaching and Learning Forum 2004, University of Washington. [http://otl.curtin.edu.au/tlf/tlf2004/debowski.html]

Department of Education, Employment and Workplace Relations. (2008a). *Review of Australian higher education: Discussion paper*. Canberra, Australia: ACT.

Department of Education, Employment and Workplace Relations. (2008b). *Review of Australian higher education: Final report*. Canberra, Australia: ACT.

Duggan, W. (2007). *Strategic intuition: The creative spark in human achievement*. New York: Columbia University Press.

Duignan, P. (2004). Forming capable leaders: From competencies to capabilities. *New Zealand Journal of Educational Leadership, 19*(2), 5–13.

Education Travel Magazine. (2008, Nov.). England government funding for NZ education. [www.hothousemedia.com (222.hothousemedia.com)]

Ewell, P. (2007). Assessment and accountability in America today. In V. Borden & G. Pike (eds.), Assessment and accounting for student learning (pp.

7–17). *New Directions for Institutional Research, Assessment Supplement 2007*. San Francisco: Jossey-Bass.

Fish, S. (2008). *Save the world on your own time*. New York: Oxford University Press.

Fullan, M. (2001). *Leading in a culture of change*. San Francisco: Jossey-Bass.

Fullan, M. (2006). *Turnaround leadership*. San Francisco: Jossey-Bass.

Fullan, M. (2008a). *The six secrets of change*. San Francisco: Jossey-Bass.

Fullan, M. (2008b). Have theory will travel: A theory of action for system change. In A. Hargreaves & M. Fullan (eds.), *Change wars*. Bloomington, IN: Solution Tree.

Gappa, J. M., Austen, A. E., & Trice, A. G. (2007). *Rethinking faculty work: Higher education's strategic imperative*. San Francisco: Jossey-Bass.

Garrett, R. (2004). The real story behind the failure of the U.K. eUniversity. *Educause Quarterly, (27)*4, 4–6.

Gay, G., & Hembrooke, H. (2004). *Activity-centered design: An ecological approach to designing smart tools and usable systems*. Cambridge, MA: MIT Press.

Gee, M. (2007). Canada must fix "pathetic" record on recruiting foreign students. *Globe and Mail Update*. [http://www.cbie.ca/data/media/news/20071101_GandM.pdf]

Gmelch, W. H. (2000). Leadership succession: How new deans take charge and learn the job. *The Journal of Leadership Studies*, 7(30), 68–87.

Gmelch, W. H. (2002). The call for department leaders. Paper presented at the annual meeting of the American Association of Colleges for Teacher Education, New York.

Gmelch, W. H., & Miskin, V. (1993). *Leadership skills for department chairs*. San Francisco: Jossey-Bass.

Goldin, C., & Katz, L. (2008). *The race between education and technology*. Cambridge, MA: Harvard University Press.

Goleman, D. (1998). *Working with emotional intelligence*. London: Bloomsbury.

Gourley, B. (2007, May). Bologna and the challenge of new technology. Speech given at the European HE Ministers meeting in London. [http://www.eua.be/eua-news/view-item/article/327/]

Gross, D. (2007, Jan. 28). The U.S. is losing market share. So what? *New York Times*. [http://www.nytimes.com/2007/01/28/business/yourmoney/28view.html]

Group of Eight. (2007, June 6). Seizing the opportunities: Designing new policy architecture for higher education and university research. G08 Discussion Paper. [http://www.go8.edu.au/storage/go8statements/2007/SUMMARY_of_Go8_paper_on_higher_education&university_research060607.pdf]

Hamilton, C. (2003). *Growth fetish*. Sydney, Australia: Allen & Unwin.

Herold, D., & Fedor, D. (2008). *Change the way you lead change*. Palo Alto, CA: Stanford University Press.

Hertzberg, H. (2008, Nov. 17). Obama wins. *New Yorker*, pp. 39–40.

Higher Education Supplement. (2007, May 30). *The Australian Newspaper*.

Homer-Dixon, T. (2006). *The upside of down: Catastrophic, creativity and the renewal of civilization*. Toronto: Knopf.

Hugo, G. (2005). Academia's own demographic time-bomb. *Australian Universities Review, 48*(1), pp. 16–23.

Hunt. D. (1987). *Beginning with ourselves*. Toronto: OISE Press.

Huntley-Moore, S., & Panter, J. (2003). Does discipline matter? Issues in the design and implementation of management development programmes for head of academic departments. Annual conference proceedings of HERDSA (Higher Education Research and Development Society of Australasia Inc.), July 2003, Christchurch, New Zealand.

Institute of International Education. (2007). International student enrollment in U.S. rebounds. [www.opendoors.iienetwork.org]

James, R. H., Bexley, E., Devlin, M., & Marginson, S. (2007). *Australian university student finances 2006*. Canberra: Universities Australia.

Jansen, J. (2008). When politics and emotion meet: Educational change in radically divided communities. In A. Hargreaves and M. Fullan (eds.), *Change war* (pp. 185–200). Bloomington, IN: Solution Tree.

Jansen, J. (in press). *Knowledge in the blood*. Palo Alto, CA: Stanford University Press.

Jaschik, S. (2007, June 25). When digital natives go to the library. Inside Higher Education Today. [http://www.insidehighered.com/news/2007/06/25/games]

Julius, D., Baldridge, J. V., & Pfeffer, J. (1999, March-April). A memo from Machiavelli. *Journal of Higher Education, 70*(2), 113–133.

Khurana, R. (2007). *From higher aims to hired hands: The social transformation of American business schools and the unfulfilled promise of management as a profession*. Princeton, NJ: Princeton University Press.

Kirp, David L. (2003). *Shakespeare, Einstein and the bottom line: The marketing of higher education*. Cambridge, MA: Harvard University Press.

Krause, K., Hartley, R., James, R., & McInnis, C. (2005). The first year experience in Australian universities: Findings from a decade of national studies. Canberra, Australia: Australian Department of Education, Science and Training.

Kuh, G., Kinzie, J., Schuh, J., & Whitt, E. J. (2005). *Assessing conditions to enhance educational effectiveness: The inventory for student engagement and success*. San Francisco: Jossey-Bass.

Larson, K., Martin, J. P., & Morris, R. (2002). Trade in educational services: Trends and emerging issues. OECD Working Paper. [www.oecd.org]

Leadership Foundation for Higher Education. (2006). *Engaging leaders in higher education: A guide to the role and work of the LFHE*. London: Author.

Levine, A. (2008). Higher education in the age of Obama. *Inside Higher Education*. [www.insidehighered.com/news/2008/11/10]

Lewin, K. (1945). *Resolving social conflicts*. New York: Harper.

Lewin, T. (2008, Nov. 8). Tough times strain colleges rich and poor. *New York Times*, Education Section. [www.nytimes.com/2008/11/08/education/08college.html]

Liker, J., & Meier, D. (2007). *Toyota talent*. New York: McGraw-Hill.

Lillis, D. (2007, May). Steering by engagement—Towards an integrated planning and evaluation framework in higher education institutes. In L. Bollaert et al., *Embedding quality culture in higher education*. European Universities Association. [http://www.eua.be/fileadmin/user_upload/files/Publications/EUA_QA_Forum_publication.pdf]

Lizza, R. (2008, Nov. 17). Battle plans. *New Yorker*, pp. 46–66.

Macilwain, C. (2007, April). The Arizona experiment. *Nature, 446*(26), 960–70.

Martin, E., Trigwell, K., Prosser, M., & Ramsden, P. (2003). Variation in the experience of leadership of teaching in higher education. *Studies in Higher Education, 28*(3), 247–259.

Massy, W., Graham, S., Short, P., & Zemsky, R. (2007). *Academic quality work: A handbook for improvement*. San Francisco: Jossey-Bass

Miller, L. (2002). *Lincoln's virtues*. New York: Vintage Books.

Mintzberg, H. (2004). *Managers not MBAs*. San Francisco: Berrett-Koehler.

Montez, J. (2003). Developing an instrument to assess higher education leadership. Paper presented at the Annual Meeting of the American Educational Research Association, Chicago, IL, April 21–25, pp. 1–20.

Moore, J. C. (2006, May). Cases of institutional transformation. *Journal of Asynchronous Learning*, [http://www.aln.org/publications/jaln/v10n2/v10n2_4cases_memb

NASPA. (2004). *Learning reconsidered: Implementing a campus-wide focus on the student experience*. Washington, DC: Author.

NASPA. (2007). *Learning reconsidered 2: Implementing a campus-wide focus on the student experience*. Washington, DC: Author. [http://www.learningreconsidered.org/]

Needham, G. (2007, June). Cited in : When digital natives go to the library. *Inside Higher Education Today*. [www.insidehighered.com]

Newman, F., Couturier, L., & Scurry, J. (2004). *The future of higher education: Rhetoric, reality, and the risks of the market*. San Francisco: Jossey-Bass.

Nimon, S. (2007). Generation Y and higher education: The other Y2K. *Journal of Institutional Research, 13*(1), 24–41.

Obama, B. (2008, Mar. 18). A more perfect union. Speech delivered in Philadelphia, National Constitution Center.

O'Meara, K., & Rice, R. E. (2005). *Faculty priorities reconsidered: Rewarding multiple forms of scholarship.* San Francisco: Jossey-Bass.

Organisation for Economic Co-operation and Development (OECD). (2000). *Education at a Glance 2001: OECD Indicators.* Paris: OECD Publishing. [http://www.mszs.si/eurydice/pub/oecd/eag2000.pdf]

OECD. (2007). *Education at a glance 2007: OECD indicators.* Paris: OECD Publishing. [www.oecd.org]

OECD (2008). *Education at a glance 2008: OECD Indicators.* Paris: OECD Publishing. [http://www.oecd.org]

Packer, G. (2008, Nov. 17). The new liberalism. *New Yorker*, pp. 84–91.

Pascarella, E., & Terenzini, P. (2005). *How college affects students: A third decade of research.* San Francisco: Jossey Bass.

Pennsylvania State University et al. (2006). Cases of institutional transformation. *Journal of Asynchronous Learning Networks, 10*(2). [www.sloan-c.org/publications/jaln/v10n2/pdf/v10n2_4cases.pdf]

Pfeffer, J., & Sutton, R. (2000). *The knowing-doing gap: How smart companies turn knowledge into action.* Boston: Harvard Business School Press.

Pfeffer, J., & Sutton, R. (2006). *Hard facts, dangerous half-truths and total nonsense.* Boston: Harvard Business School Press.

Powers, E. (2007). Profiling the American freshman. *Inside Higher Education.* [www.insidehighered.com/news/2007/01/09/freshmen]

PriceWaterhouseCoopers. (2007). Research report: The economic benefits of a degree. London: Universities UK. [www.bournemouth.ac.uk]

Ramaley, J., & Holland, B. (2005). Modeling learning: The role of leaders. In A. Kezar (ed.), *Higher education as a learning organization: Promising concepts and approaches.* San Francisco: Jossey-Bass.

Ramsden, P. (1998). *Learning to lead in higher education.* London: Routledge.

Rankin, N. (2004). The new prescription for performance: The 11th competency benchmarking survey. *Competency and emotional intelligence benchmarking 2004–2005*, IRS (LexisNexis UK).

Rappaport, A., & Creighton, S. H. (2007): *Degrees that matter: Climate change and the university*, Cambridge, MA: MIT Press.

Reeves, D. (2006). *The learning leader.* Alexandria, VA: Association for Supervision and Curriculum Development.

Remnick, D. (2008, Nov. 17). The Joshua generation. *New Yorker*, pp. 68–83.

Reserve Bank Bulletin. (2008, June). Australia's exports of education services. [222.rba.gov.au]

Robelen, E. (2008). Strategy retooled at Gates. *Education Week, 28*(13), 10–11.

Romer, P. (2004, April 18). A crisis is a terrible thing to waste. *New York Times*.

Schein, E. (1999). *The corporate culture survival guide*. San Francisco: Jossey-Bass.

Schön, D. (1983). *The reflective practitioner*. New York: Basic Books.

Scott, G. (1999). *Change matters: Making a difference in education and training*. London: Unwin.

Scott, G. (2003). Learning principals: Leadership capability and learning research in the NSW Department of Education and Training. Sydney, Australia: New South Wales Department of Education and Training. [www.det.nsw.edu.au]

Scott, G. (2006, May). Accessing the student voice: Using CEQuery to identify what retains students and promotes engagement in productive learning in Australian higher education. Canberra, Australia: Australian Government. [www.dest.gov.au]

Scott, G., Coates, H., & Anderson, M. (2008). *Learning leaders in times of change*. Sydney, Australia: Australian Learning & Teaching Council. [http://acer.edu.au/documents/UWSACER_CarrickLeadershipReport.pdf]

Scott, G., Grebennikov, L., Shah, M., & Singh, H. (2008). Improving student retention: A University of Western Sydney case study. *Journal of Institutional Research, 14*(1), 1–23.

Scott, G., & Hawke, I. (2003, June). Using an external quality audit as a lever for institutional change. *Assessment & Evaluation in Higher Education*, (28)3, 323–332.

Scott, G., & Saunders, S. (1995). The continuous learning improvement program for Australia's skill Olympians. Sydney, Australia: Workskill. [www.dsf.org.au]

Segall, P., & Freedman, G. (2007, May). Building the 21st century campus. White Paper, Blackboard Leadership Survey. [http://www.blackboard.com/clientcollateral/21st%20Century%20-%20View%20from%20the%20Top%20White%20Paper.pdf]

Smith, P. (2004). *The quiet crisis: How higher education is failing America*. San Francisco: Jossey-Bass.

Spencer, D. (2007, Dec.). Foreign student market starting to slide. *University World News*.

Spohn, W. (2003). Reasoning from practice. Syllabus narrative for the Carnegie "A life in the mind of practice" seminar. Stanford, CA: The Carnegie Foundation for the Advancement of Teaching.

Sternberg, R., & Grigorenko, E. (2007). *Teaching for successful intelligence*. Thousand Oaks, CA: Corwin Press.

Sullivan, W., & Rosin, M. (2008). *A new agenda for higher education: Shaping a life of the mind for practice*. San Francisco: Jossey-Bass.

Swail, W. S. (Spring, 2006). College student retention: Formula for student success (review). *The Review of Higher Education, 29*(3), 419–421.

Trigwell, K., Prosser, M., & Waterhouse, F. (1999). Relations between teachers' approaches to teaching and student' approaches to learning. *Higher Education, 37*(1), 57–70.

U.S. Department of Agriculture. (2007). GDP shares by country and region, historical. [www.ers.usda.gov/Data/Macroeconomics/Data/ProjectedRealGDP Shares.xls]

U.S. Department of Education. (2006). *A test of leadership: Charting the future of U.S. higher education*. Washington, DC: Author.

University Affairs Canada. (2008, May). *When students sue*. [http://www.university affairs.ca/issues/2008/may/students_sue_01.html]

Valverde, L. (2008). *Latino change agents in higher education: Shaping a system that works for all*. San Francisco: Jossey-Bass.

Vescio, J. (2005). *UTS successful graduates project: An investigation of successful graduates in the early stages of their career across a wide range of professions*. Sydney, Australia: UTS. [http://www.uts.edu.au/work/coursedevelopment/links/documents/graduateprofile.pdf]

Index